T0078445

UNLEASHED

UNLEASHED

Spread Your Wings and Fly

By

Francis Agbo

PARTRIDGE

A Penguin Random House Company

To order additional copies of this book, contact
Partridge India
000 800 10062 62
orders.india@partridgepublishing.com

www.partridgepublishing.com/india

Table of Contents

Dedication ix

Acknowledgment xi

Preface xiii

Identity..1

1   In the beginning 3

    1.1 In the beginning God... 3

    1.2 God created everything... 4

    1.3 Created by God for God 6

    1.4 Created like God... 7

    1.5 You are gods...11

2   Along came the thief..21

    2.1 Along came the thief...21

    2.2 A serpent in the garden 24

3   Along came the Christ 30

    3.1 Along came the Christ 30

4   Here come the sons of God..45

    4.1 Here come the sons of God..45

    4.2 Goldfish have no hiding place.. 48

    4.3 It's time to come to our senses...50

    4.4 Unleash the sons 53

Ability..57

5   Power and authority to unleash greatness............................59

     5.1 The LORD is with you..59

     5.2 God has given you "Doonamis"- the supernatural power of God...... 68

     5.3 God has also given you "Exousia"- spiritual authority....................75

6   On purpose with a purpose.. 80

     6.1 You are fearfully and wonderfully made 80

     6.2 Everything and everyone has a purpose..........................83

     6.3 What were you born to do? 87

     6.4 Succeed on purpose...89

Responsibility...93

7   Take responsibility 95

     7.1 You must be saved 96

     7.2 Have the faith of God 97

     7.3 Open the Book...102

     7.4 Prayer 108

     7.5 Obedience to God 111

     7.6 Dream, prepare, pursue 113

     7.7 Patience! Patience! Patience...129

     7.8 Persist till you win 133

8   Tear the leash and move forward....................................138

     8.1 Fear...139

     8. 2. Procrastination..141

     8.3. Excuses 143

9   To God be the glory.. 153

10   The conclusion of the matter...162

Dedication

This work is dedicated to God Almighty who makes all things possible and to my awesome foursome of Tosin, Kezia, Nathan and Eden. I love you LORD and I love you guys

Acknowledgment

All praise and glory goes to God Almighty who is my Heavenly Father. I love you LORD and I want to say thank you for your unmerited grace towards me. To all my mentors who have contributed the building blocks to the house that is my life over these years I say thank you. To my spiritual parents, Bishop (Dr) Fred and Bishop (Dr) Funbi Addo I say thank you a zillion times. Bishop Edwin Jarumai continues to support and encourage me as I learn under him. A big God bless you sir. I also deeply appreciate the massive input to my life by Bishop Calvin Antonza 2 and Bishop Musa Wuyep. To my beautiful wife Tosin and my kids: Kezia, Nathan and Eden what can I say? You guys are the best and my inner team. Love you loads and God bless you much. All those too numerous to mention that supported the production process for the book are recognized and much appreciated. To my sales and marketing team of Kuchali, Elizabeth and Tina, I am grateful for your zeal and the huge support you have continued to provide. God bless you too. To all the leaders and congregation at International Praise Church Abuja, Nigeria I want to say thank you for all your prayers and support. God bless you. I will not fail to appreciate my publishers Partridge Publishing Africa for a job well done and especially Grace Yap. Thanks again. All those who will read this book, be blessed, practice the principles herein and unleash the winner in them I appreciate your taking time to read and do them. Thank you.

Preface

And the angel of the LORD appeared unto him, and said unto him, The LORD is with thee, thou mighty man of valour. – Judges 6 :12

Are you tired of mediocrity, average, the status quo, the norm, or the usual? If you are then you are primed for your next level. However after you are primed for the next level you need to make yourself ready for the next level. God did not create anybody a loser or failure. God is too good to do that. God created all of us winners. Everybody can win and everybody can live a winning life and constantly too because there is a winner inside you. You are born to win but to win you must know how to win.

Gideon (meaning warrior) was born a winner but he lived life a loser. He lived averagely even though there was a winner in him. He did not know how to win. He did not know how to unleash- release the winner in him. God helped him unleash the winner in him. There is a winner warrior trapped inside everyone. You need to unleash- release the winner in you for the benefit of your world and to the glory of God. God showed Gideon how to win in life. God helped him unleash the winner warrior that was trapped inside him and his name entered God's hall of faith.

We all have a winner trapped inside us. The environment we live in with all our education, experience, past, fears, perceived or real inadequacies keeps us from being our best and doing our best. We allow self or other people imposed chains (leashes) keep us from being all that God wants us to be and doing all that God wants us to do. We stop short of true success and greatness because we keep the winner in us on a leash. God helped Gideon tear the leashes that had kept him down and he was able to unleash that winner that was lying dormant inside him.

You can be everything that God wants you to be and do everything that He wants you to do if you know how. The steps to godly success are available to all and will work for all. If Gideon succeeded and became great you too can succeed and become great. If God helped Gideon unleash the winner in him He will help you unleash the winner in you. God showed Gideon how to win continually and unleash the winner in him and He will show you too. There is a winner in you but you need to release him/her for the benefit of your world and to the glory of God. The book "Unleashed" unfolds time tested principles from the infallible and dependable word of God on how you too can unleash the winner in you.

IDENTITY

1

IN THE BEGINNING

You will never win if you never begin. – Helen Rowland

1.1 In the beginning God

In the beginning was the Word, and the Word was with God, and the Word was God. -John 1:1

In the beginning was the Word and the Word was with God and the Word was God. And so before there was ever a beginning there was God. God existed before time started. He was there before there was a beginning. He is known as the Ancient of days. That is because before time started He was there. He was before there was a beginning.

I beheld till the thrones were cast down, and the Ancient of days did sit, whose garment was white as snow, and the hair of his head like the pure wool: his throne was like the fiery flame, and his wheels as burning fire. – Daniel 7:9

Only a fool would doubt the existence or reality of an Almighty God. God has been there before the beginning. Belief that there is a supreme God is a must if you must live the kind of life He has planned for you. The bible is God's revelation to man of who God is. God has given us a revelation of Himself through the written word of God- the bible. The bible is the word of God that gives us a revelation of who God is. The bible reveals to us the nature, character, works and purpose of God. There is a God who has existed from the beginning. To acknowledge that there is a creator God is wisdom. It is foolish to believe that there is no God. God has always been and will always be. God has no beginning and He has no end. He is LORD and He is a mighty God. Daniel calls Him- the One who had been living forever.

*While I was looking, thrones were put in place. **One who had been living forever** sat down on one of the thrones. His clothes were white as snow, and his hair was like pure wool. His throne, mounted on fiery wheels, was blazing with fire, - Daniel 7:9 GNB*

In Nehemiah we are told that He alone is LORD and ruler of the universe. He is creator, owner, ruler and master over heaven and the earth and all things that are in heaven and earth. God alone remains God and He is LORD over everything and everyone.

Thou, even thou, art LORD alone; thou hast made heaven, the heaven of heavens, with all their host, the earth, and all things that are therein, the seas, and all that is therein, and thou preservest them all; and the host of heaven worshippeth thee. - Nehemiah 9:6

The heavens, earth and all that is in them did not just appear. They were created by a Supreme Being. His name is Jehovah God. He is the creator. Believe it or not there is an almighty God who existed before anything or anyone else came into existence. This God is the self-existent one. Everyone and everything else is created. He alone is not created. He is the creator. That you don't believe there is an Almighty God don't mean that there is no God. An atheist does not believe in God. He deceives himself and is foolish to say there is no God.

The fool hath said in his heart, there is no God. Corrupt are they, and have done abominable iniquity: there is none that doeth good. - Psalm53:1

It will do you good even excellently to acknowledge Him as God. It hurts you the most when you live believing there is no God. The word of God says God is real and you had better believe it for your own good. You can't hope to reach your full potential in God while doubting the existence and reality of God.

1.2 God created everything

For by him were all things created, that are in heaven, and that are in earth, visible and invisible, whether they be thrones, or dominions, or principalities, or powers:

all things were created by him, and for him: And he is before all things, and by him all things consist. Colossians 1:16-17

In the beginning God created everything. There is nothing that exists that He did not create. The theory of evolution is a lie. Any theory, idea, suggestion, thought or law that denies the existence of God is a lie. It is plain dumb or foolish for anyone to believe that this vast universe just appeared out of nothing. The universe did not just happen. God made the universe and all that is in it to happen. Chemistry, biology, philosophy or science cannot explain God or His works. Indeed as scriptures say only a fool would say there is no God.

The fool hath said in his heart, there is no God. Corrupt are they, and have done abominable iniquity: there is none that doeth good. - Psalm53:1

God is the creator of all things in heaven and on earth. The visible and the invisible. All things is all things. God created everything. Even the devil is created. He is not stronger than God. The creature cannot be stronger than the creator. Never. He is not as powerful as he has deceived the world to believe that he is. He is a created being. God is the Creator. No creature can be stronger than the Creator. There is only one supreme creator and He is LORD over the universe. He created heaven, earth and everything that is in them. His name is Jehovah God. All things in heaven and earth were created by God. The visible and the invisible things were all created by God. Principalities, thrones, powers and ALL things were created by God. Nothing and no being is stronger than God.

And, Thou, Lord, in the beginning hast laid the foundation of the earth; and the heavens are the works of thine hands: They shall perish; but thou remainest; and they all shall wax old as doth a garment. And as a vesture shalt thou fold them up, and they shall be changed: but thou art the same, and thy years shall not fail. -Hebrews 1:10-12.

God laid the foundation of the earth. The heavens, the earth and all that is them is the work of God's hands. God owns everything because God created everything. He existed before the beginning. He was been there before the beginning started but He will never grow old or weak. He remains the same. God remains God. He is not less God today than He was yesterday.

1.3 Created by God for God

And God said, Let us make man in our image, after our likeness: and let them have dominion over the fish of the sea, and over the fowl of the air, and over the cattle, and over all the earth, and over every creeping thing that creepeth upon the earth. - Genesis 1:26

God created man. Man is not the product of evolution or human philosophy, logic or thinking. Man was created by God and in the image and likeness of God. The bible says so and that settles it. We cannot know God through biology, medicine, philosophy or human knowledge. It will always be an exercise in futility for geography to try to explain creation. The word of God is the only thing that can show us who the creator is, who the creature is and what the creature can do. God is the creator of the universe. The heaven and the earth did not just happen. God created the universe.

So God created man in his own image, in the image of God created he him; male and female created he them. - Genesis 1:27.

When He wanted fish He spoke to the water. When he wanted plants He spoke to the soil but when He wanted man, He spoke to Himself. Man was taken out of God. God the Father said to God the Son and the Holy Spirit let us make man in our image.

Man was created in the image of God. God created man. It is an insult to God to say man descended from apes. You are giving the glory that belongs to God to another when you credit another with what should be credited to God. And the word of God says His glory He will not share with another. When you take the praise or adoration or the acclaim that belongs to God you have denied Him the glory. Yet God says He will not permit that His glory be given to another.

I am the LORD: that is my name: and my glory will I not give to another, neither my praise to graven images. - Isaiah 42:8

It does not matter what science and evolution say. Man was created in the image of God. God the creator created man. Man is not a descendant of apes or monkeys. Man's origin cannot be explained by the mind of man. A child can't tell who his father and mother are because he or she was not there when they were conceived. It is the father of the child that tells the child who his or her father is. The creator can't explain the account of his creation outside of the creator. Creation is trying to explain the origin of creation. It is not possible. The creator alone can explain the origin of creation and the purpose of creation. You are God's creation. He is the Potter and you are the clay.

But now, O LORD, thou art our father; we are the clay, and thou our potter; and we all are the work of thy hand. —Isaiah 64:8

Is that not so beautiful? God is my Father. I may be the clay but He is the Potter and dear friend God does not make nonsense. He does not make thrash or junk. I am the work of God's hands. God does not make mistakes. You are not a mistake. Yes we all make mistakes but just because you made a mistake does not mean you are a mistake. I am God's masterpiece. Specially designed and crafted by God Himself. Better appreciate and love you because you are God's masterpiece with value and honor. You are valuable and you are honorable because you are God's creation. Ephesians 2:10 says we are God's workmanship. We are the work of His hands. Ignore the theories of evolution, natural selection and the like. These theories are a pack of lies and the product of much thinking or imagination. You are created by God and that is the truth.

And I praise you because of the wonderful way you created me. Everything you do is marvelous! Of this I have no doubt. - Psalm 139:14 CEV

1.4 Created like God

Like God does not mean we are equal to God. We are in the same class with God. When God wanted animals He spoke to the soil. When He wanted man He spoke to Himself. God is a spirit being. Man is a triune being- a spirit that lives in a body and has a mind. The spirit of the man is the real man. The physical body of the man is the cloth or "earth suit" that clothes the spirit of man. The man is a spirit. To operate in the earth man who is a spirit needed a body so God formed a body out of dust for the spirit man. Man is thus a spirit being that lives in a body suit. When we wear clothes on our physical bodies the cloth is not our body. Our physical bodies are hidden within the cloth. Our spirit is that part of the man or woman that is created in the image of God. The body is not created in the image of God but the spirit of man is created in the image of God.

Likeness - same class of being as the Godhead. Not almighty God but we are gods. Not Almighty God but in the same class as Almighty God. In our likeness. In our class. Man was created like God. Not almighty God but in the class of gods. Man was not created equal to almighty God yet we are created in the same class like God. Like beget like. Flesh beget flesh and spirit beget spirit. Man is spirit with a body. God is spirit without a body. A body of clay was given to man to enable him live in the earth. Man is not evolved from monkeys as evolutionists will have us believe. Man came forth from God. God gave man life. Man was created in the image and likeness of God. Man who is a god was created in the same class as almighty God.

Understanding who God is and who and what He created you to be is crucial if you must be everything God wants you to become. Understanding your true identity in God is a must if you must reach your destiny or potential in God. The word of God explains who the creator is, gives us understanding of who we are, the creator's purpose for our lives and how we can fulfil His purpose for our lives. The function of a thing is closely related to its structure. Until you understand what a product is created to do by the manufacturer you cannot get the best of what it (the product) is supposed to do. That's why when a manufacturer makes a product he also includes a user's manual that describes what the product is and explains how the product functions. The manufacturer describes the various parts of the product- structure. He also describes the functions of each part so the user can derive benefit and satisfaction from the product.

Sadly what we often do is to ignore the manufacturer by ignoring the user manual. We think we know so we ignore the manufacturer's instruction. We throw away the user manual and ultimately we then pay the price when the product malfunctions or we fail to get the maximum benefit from the product. Man ignores God and fails to reach his potential only to turn around and blame God for his failure or defeat.

To live life at your best you must understand who you are. You must understand the reason you were created by the creator God. To manifest your best in God you must ask yourself - who am I. Why did God create me? To live your best you must understand your person, your God given responsibilities, abilities, strengths. Who is man? What or who am I? Your function is closely related to your identity. An eagle cannot fly (its function) if it thinks it is a chicken (structure). It will live life as a chicken if it is ignorant that it is an eagle. To be your best you must realize and live in the realization or revelation that you were created to be the best possible you that you can be and live the best possible life that you can live.

It's time to fly but you can have wings and still not be able to fly because you do not know what the wings are for. We often settle for less than God's best because we accept less of ourselves. Who is man? To understand who man is we have to ask the one who manufactured or created the man? We think we know man. We want to find meaning in life but we ignore the creator God. We think we know ourselves and so we ignore the One who created us. We don't ask Him. We don't seek Him. He understands the structure of man because He is the One that created man. We seek to live a fulfilled life but we ignore the one who is the author and sustainer of life- Almighty God.

We pursue success and satisfaction in places and things that we can't find it. God is the creator of life and all created things including man. What is God's intention or purpose for man? Why man? Who is man? We must understand God's purpose for man if we are to live the good and abundant life He has planned for us. His plan before the fall and still even after the fall is that man might live the abundant life.

The thief comes only in order to steal and kill and destroy. I came that they may have and enjoy life, and have it in abundance (to the full, till it overflows). -John 10:10 AMP

Someone has said that it is discovery that leads to recovery. An eagle can live among chickens all its life and not fly because it did not know it can fly. The day it (the eagle) discovers what its wings are meant to do it begins to fly. It's never too late to discover the life God planned for you and to live it. Abraham met God at 90 and that was when he started to live the blessed life. Moses started his journey into greatness at age 80. God is a restorer and He is able to restore the lost years. So don't dwell on the past. Don't dwell on your mistakes, failures, what has happened or not happened.

So Moses and Aaron did just as the LORD had commanded them. Moses was eighty years old, and Aaron was eighty-three when they made their demands to Pharaoh.-Exodus7:6-7NLT

At age 85 Caleb was still living the life of a winner or overcomer and conquering lands, territories, and mountains. Age is a number not an obstacle to your success and greatness. You are neither too old nor too young to become who God created you to be and to do what God created you to do. At 85, Caleb refused to settle for less than God's best for him. He grabbed God's promise for his life and refused to let go.

Now, as you can see, the LORD has kept me alive and well as he promised for all these forty-five years since Moses made this promise—even while Israel wandered in the wilderness. Today I am eighty-five years old. I am as strong now as I was when Moses sent me on that journey, and I can still travel and fight as well as I could then. -Joshua 14:10-11 NLT

Don't give in without a fight. It's not too late to "fly". It is not too late to be who God planned that you would be. It is not too late to achieve everything that God planned for you to achieve. Again age is a number and not a barrier. It is only a barrier when you allow it to stop you. Your life is not over because until God says it is over it is not over. You are never too late to succeed and become great. It's not too late to discover yourself and become everything that God created you to be. You are a son or a daughter of God and your world is waiting for you to manifest the potential or ability God put inside you. Somebody will be out of place because you did not manifest the ability God put inside you. If Moses had not manifested his potential as a leader and deliverer perhaps generations of the nation Israel would have perished in Egypt.

Friend, there is somebody that needs to hear the wisdom God has put inside you and receive direction or encouragement. Perhaps that person will commit suicide because you did not share that sermon, word of encouragement or message with them. The idea or wisdom for that invention God put inside you if acted upon would have started a company that would have offered paid employment to that man with a family of four children. But because you hoarded the idea, the product did not see the light of day. Thus the company was not started and that man did not find a job.

You sure are better than this and can do much more than you have currently done. It's time to fly and fly high. To fly however you must understand your structure or makeup. Understanding who you are is important if you must manifest your true status as a son or daughter of God. When you discover who you are in God you will not sell yourself short and settle for less. It's time to discover who we are in God so we can fly. Let us start a journey to discover who we are in God (our structure) so we can spread our wings and fly (our function). Always remember that your world is waiting for you to unleash all of who you are and what you can do for its (your world) benefit and to the glory of God. Your world has not seen your best but they will because God is set to unleash you.

To be all we must be we must have true knowledge of who God is and who we are. His purpose for us and life must be understood before you can walk in that understanding and fulfil His purpose. One wise man said where purpose is not known abuse is inevitable. The theory of evolution says man descended from monkeys or apes. Lie! Man descended from God. No theory can explain God. Theories are the products of men's mind. God is too God for the mind of man to even attempt to describe God. Man did not descend or evolve from monkeys or apes. Men descended from God. The bible tells us in God's image He (God) made man. We are created in the likeness of God and we are who He says that we are.

1.5 You are gods

I, the Most High God, say that all of you are gods and also my own children. - Psalms 82:6 CEV

The above statement is the word of God! He said- all of you are gods and also my own children. God always says what He means and means what He says. What He says is truth and no lie. You are who God says you are and you can do what the word of God says you can do. Genesis 1:27 in the Message version says God created man godlike. In the beginning we were created in His image or like Him.

If the word of God says so then it must be so. For the word of God says forever His word is settled: Psalm 119:89. - *Forever, O LORD, thy word is settled in heaven*. Again hear what the word of God says concerning you.

God created human beings; he created them godlike, Reflecting God's nature. He created them male and female. - Genesis 1:27 MSG.

Awesome! God created man like Himself. He created you godlike. We are created in His image. Dogs birth dogs. Plants reproduce plants. God Almighty reproduced or birthed gods. The spirit part of man is created like God. The real you is the unseen spirit inside the earth or clay suit that is your body. God created man as a god and a son. In the beginning and before he sinned Adam was a son of God. In the beginning before he sinned Adam was a son of God and the god of the earth. God wanted a being that will take control and rule the earth on His behalf. He created a man god and put him in the earth. Earth was not given to angels to rule. Earth was given to man (the son of God) to rule. Earth was not given to Satan to rule. Man was the god of the earth and subject only to God almighty. – Psalm 8:6

In the beginning God created man in the image of God- like God. In the beginning Adam had the life of God- eternal life. A life that cannot be destroyed. The life of God inside of Adam made man like God. He was a son of God. Adam was a son of God and he was a god in the earth. He was the son of God. A child of God is a god according to Psalm 82:6. A child of the Most High God is a god. Fish birth fish. Birds birth birds. So too God birthed gods. Children of the Most High God are gods. Religion calls it blasphemy but faith calls it the truth. You are who the word of God says you are and you can do all that the word of God says you can do. The word of God says you are a god if you are a child of the Most High God. As long as the word of God says so it is settled. You can argue with the truth but all your best efforts can't change or alter the truth.

Man was created a son of God and the god of the earth. It is only as a son that man is able to exercise his divine mandate to be fruitful, multiply and have dominion in the earth. This is how God planned it in the beginning. Man's place before sin spoiled everything was that of a son of God and a god in the earth. The word of God says ye are gods. Sons and daughters of gods are gods because they are born of God. In the garden before Adam and Eve sinned man was a god. Animals were not created to have dominion because they are not gods. Even angels including Satan- (Satan is a fallen angel) are not gods. They are even in a lower class of spirit beings than man. Man is higher in rank and authority than angels- whether they are good angels or demons. It is man that was created in the same class as God not angels. Angels are servants. They are lower in rank than man. Better believe it because only God almighty is higher in rank than man- at least in the beginning before sin came

When I view and consider your heavens, the work of your fingers, the moon and the stars, which you have ordained and established, what is man that you are mindful of him, and the son of earthborn man that you care for him? Yet you have made him but a little lower than God (or heavenly beings), and you have crowned him with glory and honor. You made him to have dominion over the works of your hands; you have put all things under his feet: - Psalm 8:3-6 AMP

Difficult for religious folk to accept this because the enemy will never want them to understand this. The enemy is a master at blinding the minds of men to the truth of the gospel for he is well aware of what knowledge of the truth can do. Truth sets free. A person is only bound when he does not know the truth. Soon as he knows the truth and believes it freedom has come and even the devil can't keep him down. Religion has been defined as the opium of the masses by someone. Might be true because religion keeps you among the mass of ignorant people, dying daily in their sins and shackled by disease, poverty, want, and all of the things that Christ died and saved us from.

Religion blinds the minds and hearts of people so they can't see and be converted to living the higher life Christ has called them to live.

For the heart of this people is waxed gross, and their ears are dull of hearing, and their eyes have they closed; lest they should see with their eyes, and hear with their ears, and understand with their heart, and should be converted, and I should heal them. – Acts 28:27

Religion keeps you bound to a set of lifeless, worthless and useless set of rules that cannot save anyone. Religion lies to us that we can never be good enough to be loved by God talk less of be called gods. It is religion that says that all we can do is try our best to keep some rules and hope God sees our best and grants us safe passage to heaven. Religion kills slowly but steadily. Religion will not accept the truth or good news that Christianity is a love relationship with God the Father who loves his people very much. Religion tries to get right with God and enslaves the religious. God's plan has always been to have sons not slaves.

He (Adam) was not a slave. Slaves don't rule. Slaves are ruled. Slaves can't exercise dominion rather they live under the dominion of another. Slaves don't decide rather others decide for them. Adam was a son of God not a slave. Adam was also a god in the earth. The life of God inside Adam made man a son of God and a god. As the God of the earth He had right and privilege from God to rule in the earth. As a son God gave man a mandate in Genesis 1:28: blessed; fruitful, multiply, replenish, subdue and have dominion.

And God blessed them, and God said unto them, be fruitful, and multiply, and replenish the earth, and subdue it: and have dominion over the fish of the sea, and over the fowl of the air, and over every living thing that moveth upon the earth. Genesis 1:28.

Be blessed

God blessed man. To be blessed means to be empowered to live the God life and the good life. To be blessed means to live life to the fullest of your God given ability and potential. That was the kind of life Adam lived in Eden. A life of faith, joy, prosperity, harmony or peace with God and with fellow man. Man was blessed and not cursed. That was man's place or status before sin came. Adam was blessed. And because he was blessed everything he did turned out successful. With God's ability and blessing upon his life, he singlehandedly named all the animals in the garden.

The amplified bible goes ahead to amplify or expand the meaning of the term blessed- happy, fortunate and to be envied.

Blessed (happy, fortunate, to be envied) is the nation whose God is the LORD, the people He has chosen as His heritage – Psalm 33:12 AMP

True and enduring happiness is a product of the blessed life. Favor is a product of the blessed life. The angel of God said to Mary- blessed are thou among women for you are highly favored. Blessed and favored. Blessed and fortunate. Blessed and happy. That was the life that Adam enjoyed. God blessed him and he was blessed.

And the angel came in unto her, and said, Hail, thou that art highly favoured, the Lord is with thee: blessed art thou among women. – Luke 1:28

When God blesses a person they are blessed and they cannot be cursed. If God calls you blessed no man or devil can say you are not blessed. God blessed Adam and he was blessed indeed. In the beginning God blessed Adam and he was blessed. The word of God says blessed is the nation (man, woman) whose God is the LORD- Psalm 33:12. Jehovah was Adam's God and so he was blessed. In the beginning before sin came in Adam was blessed.

Be fruitful

Sons of God have a divine mandate- even instruction or command to prosper and be fruitful. If you are blessed you ought to be fruitful. Sons of God are blessed and ought to be fruitful or prosperous. You are wired or designed to prosper. Adam was "wired" to prosper. He had potential- inherent or inbuilt ability to prosper. All he needed to do was to live in obedience to God and he would unleash fruitfulness from inside him. Airplanes fly because that is what they have been configured or designed by their maker to do. The mandate of the airplane is to fly. Fish are designed to swim. Birds are designed to fly. Sons of God are designed to prosper or be fruitful. God's purpose for Adam was to prosper, reproduce, fill the earth and be fruitful. Adam the son of God was designed to be fruitful (productive), multiply and have dominion in the earth. And until he sinned he did an excellent job of fulfilling his God given mandate in the earth.

Adam (man) was fruitful spiritually- for we see God come to fellowship with him in the cool of the day. Sons talk to their fathers.

That evening they heard the Lord God walking in the garden- Genesis 3:8 GNT.

He was fruitful mentally or intellectually- for it takes a mind touched by the life of God to name all the animals in the earth without the man not having attended any formal schooling.

Out of the ground the LORD God formed every beast of the field and every bird of the air, and brought them to Adam to see what he would call them. And whatever Adam called each living creature that was its name. - Genesis 2:19 NKJV

Adam was fruitful in his body for there was no sickness or disease in the garden until sin came. He did not have to battle sickness and disease. His food and water was blessed. Bacteria, viruses and other disease causing organisms did not contaminate his food and water to cause illness, sickness and disease. He lived in health

He was fruitful financially because he lived in abundance. All his need for food, air, clean portable water, gold (money) was abundantly provided in the garden by God.

And God said, "See, I have given you every herb that yields seed which is on the face of all the earth, and every tree whose fruit yields seed; to you it shall be for food. - Genesis 1:29 NKJV

The name of the first is Pishon; it is the one which skirts the whole land of Havilah, where there is gold. And the gold of that land is good. Bdellium and the onyx stone are there. Genesis 2:11-12NKJV

He was fruitful in marriage because he and his wife lived in harmony and peace. The man and the woman lived together and they were not ashamed. They were one flesh- harmony, agreement, peace and unity existed between them. Oneness and unity existed in their home.

Therefore a man shall leave his father and mother and be joined to his wife, and they shall become one flesh. And they were both naked, the man and his wife, and were not ashamed.-Genesis2:24-25NKJV

Adam the son of God who was also the god of the earth was fruitful on every side.

Multiply

To multiply means to increase in large numbers. Become great in number or to become a multitude. God said to Abraham a multitude of people shall come forth from you. He said to Abraham if you can count the sand on the seashore that is how I will make you. Can you count the grains or particles in sand? You might try but you can't for they are too many to be counted.

Man has been commanded to increase greatly. God's intention for man at the beginning was that he (man) would multiply. Multiplication means to increase greatly or abundantly. Multiplication is better and higher than addition. Addition brings increase but multiplication brings great increase. When you add twenty to twenty you get forty. But when you multiply twenty by twenty you get four hundred. That is multiplication. God's command to man was that man should multiply

God wants you to increase greatly by multiplication. Moses pronounced a blessing on the children of Israel in Deuteronomy 1:11 and said the LORD thy God multiply you a thousand times more than your fathers.

May the LORD, the God of your ancestors, make you increase a thousand times more and make you prosperous, as he promised! – Deuteronomy 1:11 GNT

You can't even begin to imagine what a 1000 times more than the blessing the fathers of faith had would mean. Abraham was blessed spiritually and materially. He had a rich relationship with God. He was also rich in cattle, silver, gold and household servants. Yet the bible says God will do for you a 1000 times more than this. Imagine what 1000 times the blessing of Solomon is. Imagine what 1000 times the blessing of the man Job would be. God said multiply and am sure not going to settle for less. Thus may the LORD God bless me a 1000 times more than He blessed Abraham, Isaac and Jacob. The LORD bless you a 1000 times more than Abraham, Isaac, Jacob and indeed all the other heroes of faith. I am sure you said amen to that.

May the LORD multiply His signs and wonders in your life a 1000 times more than He did in the life of the Old Testament saints. May He multiply His favor upon your life a 1000 times more than the favor that was upon the life of Joseph, Esther and Ruth. May He multiply His anointing upon your life a 1000 times more than the anointing that was upon Elijah and Elisha. May He multiply wisdom unto you a 1000 times more than what was inside Daniel and Solomon. The sons of Issachar had understanding of seasons and times more than all the other tribes of Israel still the LORD multiply your spiritual understanding a 1000 times more than what they had.

And of the children of Issachar, which were men that had understanding of the times, to know what Israel ought to do; the heads of them were two hundred; and all their brethren were at their commandment. - 1 Chronicles 12:32

May the LORD multiply your testimonies, breakthrough, lifting and miracles a 1000 times more than you are currently experiencing. God has not planned for you to be stagnant. He did not plan for man to merely survive. He planned for man to thrive. He did not plan for you to merely scrape through and get by. He planned for you to increase, expand, enlarge, and break limits and boundaries. He did not plan that you be diminished, decrease or become little. In the beginning He planned that you increase abundantly. Addition brings increase but multiplication brings abundant increase. You have ability in you to multiply everything God has given you or put around you. You will no longer experience decrease because from now on you will not settle for less than great increase.

You should not settle for mediocrity. You should not settle for average. You should not be content with less of God and less than what God planned for you to have. You were designed to multiply- increase abundantly, increase greatly, increase in large amounts or proportions. Being and staying small and insignificant does not bless you and it does not bless others. And most of all it does not honor or glorify God. Success honors God but failure dishonors God. Stagnancy brings death for if you are not moving forward you are alive yet dying slowly. It's in God's purpose for you to multiply and be multiplied. He even said that for the sake of Abraham He would multiply Ishmael (who was not in covenant with God) exceedingly.

And as for Ishmael, I have heard thee: Behold, I have blessed him, and will make him fruitful, and will multiply him exceedingly; twelve princes shall he beget, and I will make him a great nation. – Genesis 17:20

Is God not awesome? Imagine what it means to combine multiplication and exceeding. God will multiply you exceedingly. It's powerful that God wants you to multiply but it's something supernatural to multiply exceedingly.

God said male man and female man should multiply. I don't care where you live or who you are as long as you belong to God you will be multiplied beyond and far and above where you are now. The economy cannot stop you. The environment around you cannot stop you. The devil and hell cannot stop you from being multiplied. You shall be multiplied in your spirit, soul and body. That was God's intention in the beginning and it shall be so concerning you. You will multiply and be multiplied for so God commanded and blessed man.

Replenish the earth

Restore, refurbish, remake, repopulate, reorganize, and reorder. Man had God's blessing to restore the earth. Turn things around. Restore lost glory. The English dictionary even defines the word "replenish" as filling something that has already been emptied. If it was not working man had authority from God to restore things back to the way it originally was.

See, I have this day set thee over the nations and over the kingdoms, to root out, and to pull down, and to destroy, and to throw down, to build, and to plant. – Jeremiah1 :10

When the earth was thrown into darkness, chaos and confusion God restored light and order back to the earth. God has put the same ability in man at creation. Man could use God's ability in him (man) to restore life to dead situations.

Jesus (God in human form) restored life to dead Lazarus- *John 11*. Jesus told His disciples to raise the dead- *Matthew 10:8*. God told Ezekiel to speak to the dead dry bones- *Ezekiel 37*. Restore order. Restore creation to its original state. That is what it means to replenish the earth. As far as earth was concerned God had in the beginning given man the divine ability to replenish the earth. God destroyed the earth with flood in the days of Noah. At the end of the flood Noah came out of the ark and God empowered him to replenish or restore the earth back to the original state that the Creator planned.

And God blessed Noah and his sons, and said unto them, Be fruitful, and multiply, and replenish the earth. – Genesis 9 :1

Have dominion

You made him to have dominion over the works of Your hands; You have put all things under his feet: - Psalm 8:6 AMP

Man was created for dominion. Awesome! All things were put under his (man's) feet at creation. Under his feet is a sign of ruler ship, authority or dominion. God created the world and all that is in it. After He created the earth and all that is in it He created man and appointed him ruler, king or god of the earth. God is LORD of heaven and earth but He appointed man as governor or ruler in the earth. Satan was not the god of this world until Adam sinned. Man was the god (ruler) of the earth until he sinned and transferred that dominion or ruler ship to Satan. Until Adam sinned man was the god of this world. We see Adam ruling the earth. Everything was subject to Adam. The animals were subject to him.

He (Adam) was mandated and empowered by God to dominate the earth- Adam was appointed god or king in the earth. That is why whatever he called the animals that was the name that stood. Even Jehovah God did not change the name. God could have but He would not because He had already appointed man as king or god in the earth. And remember that where the word of a king is there is power and none can say to him what are you doing.

Where the word of a king is, there is power: and who may say unto him, what doest thou? – Ecclesiastes 8:4

Man's mandate was to exercise dominion in the earth. And he – Adam was dominating in line with his mandate. Adam was releasing all that God put on his inside. As king in the earth under God, Adam was head not the tail. He was top and not bottom. Only God was higher in rank than man. Only God was higher. Angels were not appointed king or god of the earth. Satan was not god of the earth. Man was the god (ruler) of the earth. Man's mandate was to reign in the earth. And reign he did until he sinned. Adam ruled his world. The earth was man's kingdom and man reigned as king in his kingdom. He was king of the earth. God had given man a mandate and Adam was living that mandate to the fullest. Man unleashed the best of God that God had put on his inside.

Adam the god of the earth ruled in the earth as he should. He was appointed ruler of the earth by almighty God. Man was created a son of God and the god of the earth. He was blessed, fruitful and ruling in the earth according to the mandate given him by heaven.

However something happened along the way. Someone who should have no access to Adam's earth was allowed access to the garden and the bliss and pleasure he enjoyed was soon corrupted. What was beautiful turned ugly.

2

ALONG CAME THE THIEF

The thief comes, but to steal, kill and destroy- John 10:10

2.1 Along came the thief

Everything was beautiful and excellent in the earth. God, Adam and Eve enjoyed a beautiful relationship. Man was blessed, fruitful and living the abundant life God designed for him. In heaven where God's throne was established a certain arch angel Lucifer had started a rebellion against God and failed miserably too. Some people believe there is no devil while on the other extreme some believe that he does exist and is more powerful than God. Both extremes are wrong. There is a devil but he is not as strong as he deceives the world to think he is. He is real but he is not stronger than God. Creature can never be stronger than the creator. How did he come to being? Was he always Satan?

The devil (Satan) did not start life as Satan. In the beginning he was Lucifer and not Satan. He was once Lucifer. He too is God's creation. He was created beautiful and to give God pleasure. In the beginning he (the devil) was not so. He was the anointed cherub or arch angel. As Lucifer His place was in heaven and his position was number one or chief angel. His place was in heaven at the very throne of God and he was tasked with covering the throne of God with his wings.

You were the anointed cherub who covers; I established you; you were on the holy mountain of God; you walked back and forth in the midst of fiery stones. - Ezekiel 28:14 NKJV

Along with angels Michael and Gabriel they were the chief angels in heaven.

He (Lucifer) was also in charge of praise and worship. He made beautiful music in heaven. He led praise and worship in heaven. Musical instruments- timbrels and pipes were created and given to him by the Creator God to make music in heaven. He was chief musician in heaven. He was chief of the praise makers in heaven.

You were in Eden, the garden of God; every precious stone was your covering: The sardius, topaz, and diamond, Beryl, onyx, and jasper, Sapphire, turquoise, and emerald with gold. The workmanship of your timbrels and pipes was prepared for you on the day you were created. –Ezekiel28:13NKJV

One day he started a rebellion imagining that he could overthrow the Almighty God. He wanted to dethrone God. What imagination or thinking. Why do the wicked imagine a vain thing? They imagine to do you wrong. Those that are fighting you are imagining a vain (empty, useless, unprofitable) thing. They imagine to do you harm or cause you pain yet the scriptures say that God sits in heaven and He laughs. How can you fight God and win. How can they fight you and beat you when God is with you. How can they possibly hope to triumph against you when God is on your side?

Why do the heathen rage, and the people imagine a vain thing? – Psalm 2:1

Lucifer (created) attempted to beat God (Creator) and naturally he lost woefully. After his failed rebellion he and one third of the angels were cast out of heaven.

Its tail swept away one-third of the stars in the sky and knocked them down to the earth. Then the dragon stood in front of the woman who was about to give birth so that it could devour her child when it was born. Revelation 12:4 ISV

And there was war in heaven: Michael and his angels fought against the dragon; and the dragon fought and his angels. And prevailed not; neither was their place found any more in heaven. Revelation 12:7-8

Two thirds of the angels however remained on Gods side in heaven. Lucifer and a third of the angels rebelled, lost and were expelled from heaven. Two thirds stayed loyal to God. It means that no matter what you go through there are more on your side than are against you. No matter the size of the opposition there are more with you than are against you. God's side is the winning side and if you are on God's side you are headed for victory. Two thirds is still the majority when compared to one third on the other side. More on your side means you can't be defeated. God on your side means in any situation and every circumstance you can expect to come out victorious.

Following his rebellion Lucifer and his legion of his conspirator angels were expelled from heaven.

By the abundance of your trading you became filled with violence within, and you sinned; therefore I cast you as a profane thing Out of the mountain of God; and I destroyed you, O covering cherub, from the midst of the fiery stones. "Your heart was lifted up because of your beauty; you corrupted your wisdom for the sake of your splendour; I cast you to the ground, I laid you before kings that they might gaze at you. Ezekiel 28:16-17 NKJV

Satan was cast out of heaven when he sinned. Don't be deceived for there is no place for sinners in heaven. If Satan was cast out of heaven because he sinned then anybody whether angel or man that is a sinner has no place in heaven. Color sin white all you like but there is no place for an unrepentant sinner in heaven. Sinners go to hell but saints go to heaven. Lucifer now Satan was cast out of heaven.

Instead of Lucifer the angel he became Satan the adversary, Satan the accuser, Satan the dragon, thief and destroyer. The angels that rebelled with him became demons. Instead of angels of light they became angels of darkness. Satan was looking for territory to rule. He had lost in his attempt to take authority in heaven but he was still desperate to have authority. He had lost and been expelled from heaven. Where else would he turn to he must have thought?

He could not go back to God because he had burned his bridges and so there was no way back. He told himself if legally I can't have authority, let me try and steal it. I need a place to rule. God has given man authority in the earth. I need a place to rule even if I must steal authority. And so he puts in place a plan to steal man's authority. There are only two beings that are in authority. I can't take the authority that God has. But there is man and God has given him authority in the earth. Let me see if I can take it from him says Satan.

He holds a conference with his high command and they come up with a plan on how they will steal dominion or authority from man. They are so desperate that Satan does not assign this very important task to any underling or demon. Satan takes responsibility to oversee the planning of the mission and leading the mission. It's a mission to steal authority from man. Operation steal authority is hatched and ready to be executed. They also decide that they will use the serpent as a channel.

2.2 A serpent in the garden

Meanwhile Adam the son of God and god (ruler) of the earth was busy fulfilling his God given purpose to be fruitful, multiply, replenish and have dominion over the earth. As a son of God he was living in obedience to God. He was living the blessed life and ruling the earth. He was tending the garden like God assigned him to do. His wife Eve was also helping him fulfilling his mandate in the earth. All was calm and peaceful in their garden until one day she started "fellowshipping" with some animal she should not be having fellowship with. She opened the door of her garden to a serpent.

Be careful who you allow into your garden. Everybody is not permitted in your inner space or holy of holies. There are some people you keep out of your life. You keep them outside the gates of your life. A few you allow into the gates but not into the inner court. An even fewer number you allow into the inner courts while allowing the fewest possible into the innermost courts or holy of holies of your life. Differentiate between acquaintances, friends and close friends. Some people are better outside the gates or in the outer court. Not everybody is permitted into the innermost place or holy of holies. The moment you permit those who should not be permitted into the holy of holies of your life they just might show you their true color and you may not like what you see.

Some "friends" are actually instruments in the hands of the enemy to destroy that dream God has given you. Some have lost their marriages because they allowed a serpent who looked like a friend into their garden. Someone's child started doing drugs because they talked to another kid who turned out to be a "serpent". They accommodated the serpent and the serpent was used by the enemy to destroy what God has given to them to be a blessing. You don't need everybody in your life and you sure don't need to be friends with everybody. Joseph learned the hard way that it is not everybody that you open your mouth and share your dreams with. Some people are weapons in the hands of the enemy to kill your dreams.

And when they saw him afar off, even before he came near unto them, they conspired against him to slay him. And they said one to another, Behold, this dreamer cometh. Come now therefore, and let us slay him, and cast him into some pit, and we will say, some evil beast hath devoured him: and we shall see what will become of his dreams. – Genesis 37:18-20

Satan by this time was desperately looking for a place to rule. He wanted a place to rule and be in charge. That was the reason he was thrown out of heaven in the first place. He wanted to rule or be in charge. He had been expelled from heaven but his desire to rule or be in charge had not changed. He said to himself- well if I can't usurp (overthrow) God's authority let me see if I can usurp authority from the one God gave authority in the earth. If I can't overthrow Almighty God let me see if I can overthrow the one God gave authority in the earth- the man god. Remember that the son of God is a god. As sons of God, man had been given authority to rule as god in the earth. Satan desired to rule so bad that he was willing to do anything.

One day in the garden we find Eve in deep conversation with the serpent. What was she doing talking to a serpent? And what was Adam doing sitting and watching her talk to the serpent and doing nothing about it. Rather than chatting with the serpent they should have been casting or driving the serpent out of the garden. Rather than listen to someone plant doubt concerning what God had told Adam they should have been casting down every imagination that exalts itself against the knowledge of God.

Casting down imaginations, and every high thing that exalteth itself against the knowledge of God, and bringing into captivity every thought to the obedience of Christ. – 2 Corinthians 10:5

Someone's life has not made much progress because there are some serpents that appear to be friends in his or her garden. You are heeding and following the advice of the wrong people. Not everybody should travel with you on the road to your dreams. Some people are excess baggage you can't afford to carry as you move towards your dreams. One wise man said when you allow the right person into your life right things start happening to you but if you allow the wrong person access to your life wrong things start happening to you. Eve allowed the wrong "creature" access to her life and it caused her great loss.

The serpent was in reality an instrument in the hands of the devil to steal man's God given authority or right to rule. This is earth. As God seeks to use men so too the devil seeks to use men. As God seeks to use men as instruments or channels for good so too the devil seeks to use men as instruments for evil. The devil influenced and used the serpent to bait and deceive Eve. The first place he starts is to twist the word of God that man has heard. The enemy always attempts to twist the word of God that you have heard. He is still doing the same even today. He gets men to doubt the word of God. He is always out to destroy your faith in God and in the promises of God. Hear what the serpent said to Eve:

Now the snake was the most cunning animal that the Lord God had made. The snake asked the woman, "Did God really tell you not to eat fruit from any tree in the garden?" - Genesis 3:1 GNT

Eve entered a discourse or conversation with the serpent. She debated God's word with the devil. The word of God remains the word of God. Always true yesterday, today and forever. Hear what she said to the serpent:

"We may eat the fruit of any tree in the garden," the woman answered, "except the tree in the middle of it. God told us not to eat the fruit of that tree or even touch it; if we do, we will die."- Genesis 3:2-3 GNT.

Finally the serpent (still influenced by the devil) convinces her and Eve eats fruit of the tree that God had said don't eat. The laws of God are not established to deny you rather they are there to protect you. Obedience has reward while disobedience has consequences. She ate the fruit and also gave to Adam to eat. Satan and hell just won a battle- not the war. All temptation that the enemy brings your way is a battle. Fight to win. Adam and Eve had just lost a battle. Like the word of God had promised they died- cut off or separated from God. It was a spiritual death. Their spirits inside them died even though they were still physically alive.

Sin came into the world through one man, and his sin brought death with it. As a result, death has spread to the whole human race because everyone has sinned. - Romans 5:12 GNT

Sin brought death. God created man and gave him life. Man was infused with the God kind of life at creation. This life is called eternal life- the nature of God. When man sinned he lost that nature and inherited death- the nature of the devil. The nature of God in man died. A mystery but true. Without the life of God or eternal life man is lost both now and in eternity. Man cannot realize his full potential while in that state of death. Death and darkness became man's master after Adam sinned.

Have you ever wondered why it is easy for one to live in sin and even enjoy living in sin? The nature of sin entered inside man right from the day Adam sinned. The bible says death passed onto all men the day Adam sinned. We are born in sin. We are born with the sin nature- death. And when you have the nature of a thing it comes naturally for you to do according to your nature. A bird does not pray before it flies for the ability to fly has been built into its nature. Airplanes fly because it is natural or in their nature to fly. Don't ask a dog or cow to fly for it is not part of its nature. What is not in the nature of a thing will not be natural for the thing to do. It will struggle to live contrary to its nature.

Man sins and quite easily too because he has the nature of sin. Sin enslaves. Sin makes slaves out of men. Hear what Paul said

For that which I do I allow not: for what I would, that do I not; but what I hate, that do I. - Romans 7:15

Sin is a force. Sin is a slave driver. Anyone under the control or rule of sin can't help himself or herself. You need a higher force to dislodge it. Again hear what the apostle had to say

O wretched man that I am! Who shall deliver me from the body of this death? - Romans 7:24 KJV

Satan succeeds in deceiving Eve and sin gains control. They ate from the tree that God had commanded Adam that he should not eat from. They disobeyed God and obeyed Satan. Satan had hatched a plan and he had succeeded with his plan. The moment they obeyed Satan sin had entered the garden. Sin brought death too. And very importantly they transferred their authority to Satan. From being sons of God they became slaves of Satan.

Sin brought a curse on mankind. Instead of blessed (fortunate, happy, empowered by God) man was now cursed (doomed, enslaved, frustrated, weak). Instead of ruler man was now the ruled. Sin always has consequences. No matter how much men try to paint it beautiful, sin has consequences. You can't play with sin and not get hurt. Sin promises so much yet delivers so little. It may look good to the eyes, desirable to be had just like the apple but it has consequences. The bible tells us that the wages of sin is death.

For the wages of sin is death; but the gift of God is eternal life through Jesus Christ our Lord. - Romans 6:23

Sin has wages. Sin brought death to man. What is death? Separation. Adam was cut off from God and the life (power) of God the day he sinned. Remember what God told them in Isaiah 58. He said it is not my hand that is short. Rather it is your sins that have separated you from my power.

Behold, the LORD'S hand is not shortened, that it cannot save; neither his ear heavy, that it cannot hear. But your iniquities have separated between you and your God, and your sins have hid his face from you, that he will not hear. – Isaiah 59:1-2

Sin brought death to mankind. Sin brought a curse. God cursed man. Until sin came man was blessed. When sin came man was cursed by God. Sin made man subject to Satan. Instead of reigning as a king man became a slave to Satan.

The son of God became a slave. He was no longer the god of this world. He yielded or seeded that position to Satan. In the beginning before sin Adam had been infused or injected with the very life of God- eternal life. When he sinned he lost eternal life (the nature of God) and inherited the nature of the devil- death. God had warned him that the day he eats the apple he would die. And so it proved. Death now reigned over him. The son of God was now a slave.

Man who was created a ***son*** and a god was now a ***slave*** to sin. Instead of the ***ruler*** he was now the ***ruled***. He was ***blessed*** but after he sinned he is now ***cursed***. In his sinful nature he could no longer rule in the earth as a king and god. He could not live the abundant life God designed for him. Sin had corrupted and distorted the potential of man. Satan the thief had succeeded in stealing authority from man. Where life once reigned death now reigned. Man could not fulfil his full potential in God. In place of fear there was now fear, doubt and anxiety. A leash or cap had been put on man's potential or ability. He could not live life to the fullest as God planned it. Sin had capped man's inherent ability. Man had fallen short of the glory of God and till today sinful man is still falling short of the glory of God.

But was God just going to sit back and do nothing? Certainly not. He was not going to leave man in this condition. God loved man and He was determined to do something about man's condition.

3

ALONG CAME THE CHRIST

Christ is the bread for men's souls- Ian Maclaren

3.1 Along came the Christ

He loves us, and by his sacrificial death he has freed us from our sins and made us a kingdom of priests to serve his God and Father. To Jesus Christ be the glory and power forever and ever! Amen. - Revelation 1:6 GNT

God loves man! What is sinful man that God would love him? Man sinned yet God did not cast man away. He loves man. Man had sinned and God placed a curse on man. Still God loved man and even in the face of fulfilling the demands of divine justice God still had a plan to redeem man. Man had failed but God refused to leave man in that place of failure. God loves us. Even better God loves me. God loves you. God don't like the sin but He loves man.

God's plan was to save man. Yes man had failed but no, God would not leave man that way. And He revealed His intention when He spoke in the Garden of Eden:

And I will put enmity between thee and the woman, and between thy seed and her seed; it shall bruise thy head, and thou shalt bruise his heel. - Genesis 3:15

Who is this seed that will bruise the head of the serpent (symbol of Satan)? The seed is the only begotten Son of God called Christ.

And he laid hold on the dragon, that old serpent, which is the Devil, and Satan, and bound him a thousand years, - Revelations 20:2

God planned that He would send the Christ to bruise the head of the serpent who is the devil.

Now to Abraham and his seed were the promises made. He saith not, and to seeds, as of many; but as of one, and to thy seed, which is Christ. – Galatians 3:16

Christ is the seed of the woman that came and successfully bruised the head of the serpent- Satan to set man free from the bondage of sin and death. And boy did He bruise the head of the enemy of our souls. He- Christ was born of a virgin and came to the earth to save the world from sin. Christ's chief mission on earth was to save man from sin.

This is a faithful saying, and worthy of all acceptation, that Christ Jesus came into the world to save sinners; of whom I am chief. -1 Timothy 1:15

Christ brought salvation to the world. He is the promised seed that God sent to redeem man from sin and death. There is no other name that has been given under heaven by whom men would be saved other than the name of Jesus.

Neither is there salvation in any other: for there is none other name under heaven given among men, whereby we must be saved. – Acts 4:12

The biggest enemy of man is not the devil. Man's biggest enemy is sin. Sin brought death. Sin is the root of **ALL** sickness, disease, divorce, poverty and every other evil. All the social programs the world has invented are good but they are only dealing with the symptoms not the roots. Until the root is dealt with men will still struggle to reach their full potential in God. Christ came that He might destroy Satan, sin and its power over us and He succeeded.

Forasmuch then as the children are partakers of flesh and blood, he also himself likewise took part of the same; that through death he might destroy him that had the power of death, that is, the devil. - Hebrews 2:14

What a mighty yet loving God we serve. I hope as you read this you know Him as your God and Savior. If you don't, you are missing so much but there is hope for you even now. Christ is the Savior of the world and there is no other.

The next day John seeth Jesus coming unto him, and saith, Behold the Lamb of God, which taketh away the sin of the world. - John 1:29

Christ came into the world to take away the sins of the world and He did so. He came that He might destroy death and him who had the power of death. Satan came to steal, kill and destroy but Christ came that we might have life and have it more abundantly.

Christ came to the world to save man from the power of Satan and sin. He came to redeem us. He came to transform us from slaves to sons and daughters of the Most High God. All who by faith accept His sacrifice on the cross become adopted sons and daughters of God. They become kings to reign in this life and to be with Him in eternity. The power of sin and Satan is broken. Satan came to steal, kill and destroy but the son of God came that we might have life and have it more abundantly. Christ the Messiah came that we might be saved from sin and to live life as it was in Eden before sin entered the garden. And now all those who receive Christ's free gift of salvation are:

- Cleansed from sin and forgiven
- Redeemed
- Blessed not cursed
- Empowered to live and rule as kings

We are cleansed from sin and forgiven

I am writing to you, little children, because for His name's sake your sins are forgiven [pardoned through His name and on account of confessing His name.-1 John 2:12 AMP.

Sin was a barrier or obstacle between man and God until Christ the Savior came and paid the price for sin. When we turn to God in repentance, confess our sins we receive forgiveness. The obstacle called sin is removed. We are cleansed. We are forgiven. Sin or death is removed from our spirits and our spirits are made alive by God. We receive eternal life once we turn to Christ. We are no more enemies with God. We have peace with God. We become His beloved children again. We are adopted into the family or household of God where Christ is the firstborn.

Indeed along came the Christ to take away the sins of the world.

We are reconciled back to God- we have peace with God and from God. The wall of separation between us and God has been pulled down. We are no more enemies of God. We are beloved children of God now that our sins have been forgiven. We are saints of God. We are friends of God. We are God's chosen people. A new creation.

We are redeemed

For the LORD hath redeemed Jacob, and ransomed him from the hand of him that was stronger than he. - Jeremiah 31:11

The devil brought sin, death and bondage. We were held ransom by darkness but Christ paid with His blood to ransom us back to God. He has redeemed us from the power of Satan and hell. We could not save ourselves. The enemy was too strong for us but God always is the strongest. He redeemed us from sin and death. To redeem something or someone means to buy back. It means to pay a price and obtain something. Christ paid with His precious blood to redeem man back to God.

*And they sung a new song, saying, Thou art worthy to take the book, and to open the seals thereof: for thou wast slain, and hast **redeemed** us to God by **thy blood** out of every kindred, and tongue, and people, and nation; - Revelations 5:9*

We are redeemed and the price that was paid for our redemption was the Blood of Jesus. His death gave us life. As sinners we were slaves in the kingdom of darkness but once we accept the free gift of salvation we are translated out of the kingdom of darkness into the kingdom of light. We are redeemed- we don't belong in the kingdom of darkness anymore. We have been translated out of the kingdom of darkness into the kingdom of light. Darkness does not have the power to rule over us anymore for we are not citizens of that kingdom.

Who hath delivered us from the power of darkness, and hath translated us into the kingdom of his dear Son- Colossians 1:13

The king of the kingdom of darkness has no power over us because we are not his subjects. We have been removed from the kingdom of darkness so he has no right or authority to rule over us. Satan is not the boss of the believer in Christ. God is the LORD of the believer and so Satan can't lord anything over the believer except through ignorance on the part of the believer. We have been redeemed and we will declare so because the word of God says that let the redeemed of the LORD say so. Bought (purchased) with His precious blood.

Take heed therefore unto yourselves, and to all the flock, over the which the Holy Ghost hath made you overseers, to feed the church of God, which he hath purchased with his own blood.- Acts 20:28

You are who God says you are and you can do all things that God says you can do. You have been redeemed by God. Paid for by God. You don't belong to Satan anymore. There is a tag or mark on you that has been inscribed with His blood and it says **SOLD**. The sign upon your life reads- **GOD'S PROPERTY! NOT FOR SALE**. There is a mark on you and it reads touch not mine anointed. You have been redeemed from darkness and hell. Sin and Satan have no dominion over you except you let them through ignorance or you continue to willfully live in sin after you have been saved. Along came Christ to redeem you.

You have been redeemed. Declare it. Accept it that you are redeemed. Let the redeemed of the LORD say so

Let the redeemed of the LORD say so, whom he hath redeemed from the hand of the enemy- Psalm 107:20

You are blessed not cursed

Sin brought a curse on man. Christ came and paid the price for our sins that we might no more be cursed but blessed.

Christ hath redeemed us from the curse of the law, being made a curse for us: for it is written, Cursed is every one that hangeth on a tree. That the blessing of Abraham might come on the Gentiles through Jesus Christ; that we might receive the promise of the Spirit through faith. - Galatians 3:13-14

He took the curse that was upon our lives and gave us His blessing. We are no longer cursed. We are blessed for life. We are now too blessed to be cursed. The believer is blessed by God and can't be cursed by anyone. We have moved from the realm of the cursed to the realm of the blessed. He (Christ) became cursed that we might be blessed. I can shout it loud that I am blessed. Indeed I am blessed for the word of God calls me blessed.

Blessed be the God and Father of our Lord Jesus Christ, who hath blessed us with all spiritual blessings in heavenly places in Christ- Ephesians 1:3

Romans 4:7 AMP translation declares that those who have had their sins forgiven are blessed, happy and to be envied.

Blessed and happy and to be envied are those whose iniquities are forgiven and whose sins are covered up and completely buried- Romans 4:7 AMP

You have been forgiven because of what Christ did for you on the cross. You are no longer cursed. You are blessed. He became cursed that you might be blessed. Your past with all your sins, mistakes, errors and the like have been buried. You are blessed because of what Christ did for you when He died for your sins.

We will live and rule like kings

Death ruled like a king because Adam had sinned. But that cannot compare with what Jesus Christ has done. God has treated us with undeserved grace, and he has accepted us because of Jesus. And so we will live and rule like kings. - Romans 5:17 CEV

Death ruled after Adam sinned. Now because of what Christ has done we will live and rule like kings. Sin made us slaves of Satan. Christ died for our sins that we might be restored as kings and sons of God and we will reign. The devil has been stripped of authority. The authority he stole from man has been restored back to man by Christ.

And having spoiled principalities and powers, he made a shew of them openly, triumphing over them in it. - Colossians 2:15

Our salvation was completed on the cross and by His blood we have been restored to our original status of gods in the earth. We will rule and have dominion over the whole earth.

And hast made us unto our God kings and priests: and we shall reign on the earth. - Revelation 5:10

We refuse to live mediocre and average lives anymore for we have been redeemed and are now kings and priests. We will live the abundant life God planned for us. We refuse to live like slaves because we are no more slaves but sons of the Most High God. We are born again to rule. As sons of God we will reign. We will possess our possession and inheritance in God. Redeemed man is destined to reign and we will reign. Born again man will reign in this life. We are not waiting to get to heaven before we rule and reign. We will rule and reign here and now for we are born to reign. God designed man to live an abundant life. Anything short of it is not the will of God and you must resist it.

Salvation is something everyone who desires to become everything God wants them to become must first experience. Salvation gives God the permission to transform your whole life. When you accept the free gift of salvation you have positioned yourself for transformation of your whole life. Salvation through Christ is a must if you must experience transformation. See what He did to the first disciples who later became the 12 apostles. He gave them a proposition- Come follow me and I will make you. They followed Him throughout His ministry in the earth and even after he departed the earth. Their lives were so relevant to their generation that it was written concerning them in Acts 17:6

And when they found them not, they drew Jason and certain brethren unto the rulers of the city, crying, these that have turned the world upside down are come hither also- Acts 17:6

They turned the world upside down in a positive manner. In the beginning they were mere village fishermen but after they met Jesus they were empowered to unleash the grace or anointing of God that was upon their lives. They met Jesus and He transformed their lives and they went on to transform their world.

Do you want to unleash that hidden person (the real you) that God created you to be? Do you want to unleash greater levels of success, joy, prosperity and ultimately greatness from your life? You desire right if your answer is yes. You must be saved. You need to accept the gift of salvation that is found only in Christ. Every man that is not saved is a slave to sin. And slaves don't reign. No matter how much fame and fortune you have achieved as a slave you are still a slave. And you have only just scratched the surface of the potential that God has put inside of you. You have not started to reign if you are not saved for you are still a slave. All unredeemed men are slaves and slaves can't reign.

Only kings reign. That is why Christ came to redeem us and make us into a kingdom of priests that we might serve God and reign in the earth.

He loves us, and by his sacrificial death he has freed us from our sins and made us a kingdom of priests to serve his God and Father. To Jesus Christ be the glory and power forever and ever! Amen. - Revelation 1:6 GNT

Space and time will not permit us to describe the full extent of what God did for man through Christ. Suffice to say that man was held bondage by sin. Man had fallen short of the glory of God. Man was condemned to death, cursed and suffering the evil effects of sin. Man needed a redeemer. A redeemer is someone who buys back something. God loved us and He purchased us with the priceless blood of His Son. We are bought with a price. Bought by the blood and now we can reign as kings here on earth.

The first Adam made man slaves of sin and Satan. The second Adam- Christ made us sons of God. The second Adam made us heirs of God. We are born again into a new inheritance in God. He changed our destiny for life. From hopelessness to hope. From failure to success. From no future to a glorious future. We have been translated out of darkness into light. Satan and sin do not lord it over us. We lord it over Satan and sin because of what Christ has done for us.

Behold, I give unto you power to tread on serpents and scorpions, and over all the power of the enemy: and nothing shall by any means hurt you. - Luke 10:19

We are sons of the kingdom and Jehovah is our God and Father. From not been able to call Him Father we can now from our hearts call Him our Father. Satan is the father of those that are in the world but he is not the father of those that are in Christ.

Ye are of your father the devil, and the lusts of your father ye will do. He was a murderer from the beginning, and abode not in the truth, because there is no truth in him. When he speaketh a lie, he speaketh of his own: for he is a liar, and the father of it. -John 8:44

The believer is in the world but He is not of the world. We have received the spirit of God not the spirit of the world. The greater one lives in us. God has made His home in us for life. We are in Christ. We are seated with Christ in heavenly places far and above all principality and power.

Far above all principality, and power, and might, and dominion, and every name that is named, not only in this world, but also in that which is to come. And hath put all things under his feet, and gave him to be the head over all things to the church- Ephesians 1:21-22

We are now light and can't be beaten by darkness. Darkness cannot thrash light. Darkness cannot overcome light. Darkness cannot beat light. Darkness is certainly no match for light. Darkness does not drive away light. Rather light will beat darkness any day. Light remains stronger than darkness all the time. Satan and sin (darkness) does not reign over the believer any more. We will reign and rule because we are now light and darkness should not rule over us

The light shines in darkness and the darkness has never put it out- John 1:5 GNT

The dominion of Satan and every work of darkness is broken. Christ has disarmed darkness. Darkness and the agents of darkness can rule in the life of those who are in the world but for the believer in Christ it is not so. We are light and darkness should not have dominion over us. Darkness will only reign or have dominion in the life of the believer when he or she is ignorant of who they are in Christ. It is ignorance that makes light to run from darkness. Being ignorant is being in darkness. And when you are ignorant of who you are in God then darkness will reign and run riot in your life.

You shall know the truth and the truth shall set you free. Not knowing the truth will keep you in bondage to what you have been made lord or master over. The lion may be king of the jungle and still be intimidated by smaller animals if it don't recognize and live in the reality or knowledge that it is the king of the jungle. The lion may be the strongest of the animals in the wild and still be intimidated by weaker animals because it don't know who or what it is. The beast that lacks understanding of what it is will perish. In the kingdom there are believers living beneath God's design for their lives because they know not. Liberty has come and you are set to be unleashed on your world. Your world has not yet seen what God can do with you and through you but they are about to.

But as it is written, Eye hath not seen, nor ear heard, neither have entered into the heart of man, the things which God hath prepared for them that love him. - 1Corinthians 2:9

Welcome to your new world and to the new you. You are set to break records, smash barriers and limitations so that you can be the best that God wants you to be and to be all He wants you to be. It is time to unleash the sons of God on the earth. Are you ready for transformation?

Salvation in Christ is a must for transformation

Salvation is to be found through him alone; in all the world there is no one else whom God has given who can save us. - Acts 4:12 GNB

When Adam sinned he lost the nature or life of God and inherited the nature of Satan- death. He lost the ability to reign in life. His potential or God given abilities became stunted. He could no longer perform to the level that God planned that he would perform. Sin brought death- separation from God. Sin cost man eternal life. Sin brought death. Sin cost Adam his place. Sin cost Adam his Eden. But thank God for Christ. He restored man back to God. Christ restored man back to his original position of fruitfulness, success and dominion.

Before sin came Adam was a king reigning or exercising dominion in the earth. Adam was a son of God but when he sinned he became a slave to Satan. Christ paid the price for sin and made it possible for man to become a son of God again. Sons that would take their place in the earth as sons of God to reign (rule) in the earth. Sons who will be instruments in the hand of God to thrash darkness and enforce God's will and plan in the earth.

Sin disconnected man from God. To rediscover meaning, achievement and greatness man needs to reconnect back to God. Without Him you can do nothing. Without him all your achievements or successes are insignificant compared to what you could have achieved with Him. You have only scratched the surface of the potential He put inside you if you have reached a certain level of achievement without Him in your life.

Christ paid with his life that we might receive eternal life again. Without the life of God you cannot reign. Without eternal life which is the nature of God we cannot fulfil our full potential. Eternal life is divine fuel that powers your life so that you can reign in life. Without the life of God men remain trapped and unable to become what God wants them to be. The salvation experience is more than that you are saved and going to heaven to be with the LORD someday soon or later. Until that day there is a life to be lived. There are lives to be touched for God. Your world is crying out to be liberated from the bondage of sin and Satan. And in these last days it is the sons of God that will be God's instruments to liberate their world.

For the earnest expectation of the creature waiteth for the manifestation of the sons of God. – Romans 8:19

All willing and obedient sons and daughters of God will need to take their place in the world to be deliverers for God. Christ died so that all those who accept the free gift of salvation might receive power to be called sons of God and live the life that God designed them to live. A life of righteousness, peace, joy and power. Men were saved so that when they accept God's free gift of salvation they would taste the supernatural power of God and also be channels of the supernatural power of God. Our God is raising deliverers in Zion (the Church) in our day who will be instruments of victory and deliverance in their world.

Deliverers will assemble on Mount Zion to judge Esau's Mountain, and to the LORD will the kingdom belong – Obadiah 1:21 ISV

Sadly many of God's children are still living beneath the potential of God for our lives due to ignorance and fear. Sons of the kingdom though sons with power and authority, are still living like slaves. Though they are sons they are still oppressed by what they should be oppressing and thrashing. According to King Solomon it is an error for sons to live like slaves.

There is an evil which I have seen under the sun, as an error which proceedeth from the ruler. Folly is set in great dignity, and the rich sit in low place. I have seen servants upon horses, and princes walking as servants upon the earth. – Ecclesiastes 10:5-7

To unleash God's full potential in your life you must first become that person that God designed you to be. To become that successful and great person God wants you to be you must first be reconciled to God by accepting Christ as your Lord and Savior. That's the first step. The prodigal son cannot live like the king's son that he is while he is cut off from the father and living in a faraway country of sin. He needs to return home and be reconciled to the father then all of his privileges and rights as a son can then be restored to him. He can now live the life that the father planned for him.

And am no more worthy to be called thy son: make me as one of thy hired servants. And he arose, and came to his father. But when he was yet a great way off, his father saw him, and had compassion, and ran, and fell on his neck, and kissed him. – Luke 15:19-20

God has been waiting for you to return home. Every person who has not been reconciled to God is a son that is living in a far country. God stands at the door of your heart knocking and waiting for you to open the door of your heart so he can come dwell in your heart and sup (eat, fellowship) with you and you with Him.

Behold, I stand at the door, and knock: if any man hear my voice, and open the door, I will come in to him, and will sup with him, and he with me. - Revelation3:20

Like the father of the prodigal son, God has been looking out through the window expecting you to return home from that faraway land of sin. Sin stunts a man's potential and He cannot fulfil Gods purpose for his life. Sin is a reproach but righteousness exalts a nation. Sin keeps you under but righteousness lifts you to that higher life God has called you to live. Be reconciled to God if you want to become that person God wants you to become.

When you accept and invite God into your heart he injects eternal life into your spirit. Your spirit comes alive and is reconnected back to God and you can bear much fruit. John 15:5 tells us that He is the vine and we are the branches.

I am the vine, ye are the branches: He that abideth in me, and I in him, the same bringeth forth much fruit: for without me ye can do nothing- John 15:5

As long as the branch is connected to the vine it draws life, power, energy and grace from the vine and it will be fruitful and fulfil its full potential. But if the branch is disconnected from the vine it is disconnected from life and it cannot bear fruit. It cannot be useful for anything other than to be thrown into the fire – John 15:6.

If a man abide not in me, he is cast forth as a branch, and is withered; and men gather them, and cast them into the fire, and they are burned.

Anyone that has not received salvation in Christ is a sinner. His spirit or inner man inside him is dead. And because his spirit inside him is dead all the potential or ability- ideas, wisdom, inventions, products, talent etc. lie buried and largely untapped. He cannot release or unleash that potential to the fullest. He may scratch the surface and release some of it but he cannot release all of it. He can only release most if not all of it when He accepts Christ into his life and Christ releases eternal life into his life and causes his spirit to come alive. With the life of God inside him that person is now infused with power to unleash the potential of God deposited in him. He can now release success and greatness buried inside him.

Christ told the religious leaders of his day that except you are born of the spirit of God you cannot see- experience kingdom signs, wonders and miracles. You are cut off from being a sign and a wonder and doing signs and wonders if you are not born again by the Spirit of God. Many people today are still playing religion. Going to church yes but denying the power thereof.

Having a form of godliness, but denying the power thereof: from such turn away. – *2 Timothy 3:5*

The sinner has not received Christ and so they have not received that eternal life from God that is able to transform their lives and give them a future in this here life and save them from eternal damnation and separation from God in the life hereafter. The enemy is comfortable with people practicing religion as long as they are denying the power thereof. He is happy with you going to church every Sunday and struggling to keep a few man-made rules as long as you do not experience the power of the gospel and experience the transformation only God can produce in your life.

He is comfortable as long as like Nicodemus we sit and argue that all of this "born again" stuff is not real so that he (Satan) can keep you down and bound.

He is very happy for you to remain a slave to him by remaining tied to religion. Religion never saved anyone and it can never save anyone. It is the power of God that saves and transforms. Religion will still keep you bound to sin and keep you from releasing your full potential in God.

For I am not ashamed of the gospel of Christ: for it is the power of God unto salvation to everyone that believeth; to the Jew first, and also to the Greek.- Romans 1:16

Step out of religion and embrace the eternal life that Christ came that all who would receive Him might experience. When you experience eternal life your life will experience supernatural transformation. Your journey towards releasing success and greatness starts when you receive Christ. When you receive Christ you receive eternal life - spiritual energy or might that is able to move you to the level that God planned for you. Eternal life in Christ empowers you for a life of success and greatness. Eternal life will release that person that God created you to be and ultimately cause the release of all the enormous potential God planted inside you for the good of your world and to the glory of God. It's time to release that person that God planned that you would be so that you can unleash your potential to the world and bring glory to God.

You will only find true fulfilment when you find your God given purpose in life. And you will only find your God given purpose when you reconnect with the God who designed your purpose. Every sinner is disconnected from God and needs to reconnect back to God if they are to live the abundant life of power, success and greatness He planned for them. If you are not saved you can't unleash the fullness of God that has been deposited inside you. Salvation is a must for true transformation to take place

To release the power, success and greatness God planned for you, you must first become the person God planned for you to be. To unleash that potential He has planted inside you there is need for you to become the person He wants you to be. The structure of a thing is very much related to its function. To function the way God will have you to function you must develop into the person God created you to be. Discover the real you. That hidden person inside you. To discover who the creature is, the creature must be reconciled to the Creator. You must be reconciled to God. Are you ready for transformation? If you are then there must first be reconciliation. If you want to reconcile yourself back to God all you need to do is say the following prayer and believe it from your heart.

Father in heaven I am a sinner. I repent of my sins. Forgive me, cleanse me from sin, make me your child and fill me with your Holy Spirit in Jesus Name. Amen. Thank you for forgiving me my sin and making me your child.

Congratulations on your new birth. You are now a child of God. The next thing to do is for you to get a bible and start to read daily. A line from one old Sunday school hymn says- *Read your bible, pray every day.* Yes read your bible and pray every day. Also pray that God will lead you to a bible believing church close to you where you can submit to the pastor and grow in the faith.

4

HERE COME THE SONS OF GOD

*Wherefore thou art no more a servant, but a son; and if a son, then an heir of God through Christ. – **Galatians 4:7***

4.1 - Here come the sons of God

For the earnest expectation of the creature waiteth for the manifestation of the sons of God. - Rom 8:19

We have entered the days of the manifestation of the sons of God. The sons of men have been held bound by sin and are under the dominion of Satan. The sons of God on the other hand are those who have been set free from sin and are walking in their God given power and authority. God's plan has always been to liberate the world from the bondage of sin and death. And in these last days before Christ returns God will use vessels of clay called the sons of God. Blood bought, saved and redeemed sons and daughters of God. Spirit men filled with the life of God even though clothed with vessels of clay. They are vessels of clay in which He has deposited divine ability, might or strength.

God the creator is not pleased to see the creation held bound by sin and Satan. He is a good God who causes His rain to rain upon both the righteous and the wicked. He loves the sinner even though He does not love sin. The creator God wants the creation to be set free from the corruption or death caused by sin but He will use vessels- sons of God to do just that. The whole of creation has been groaning and looking to be set free by the power of God.

For we know that the whole creation groaneth and travaileth in pain together until now. - Rom 8:22

Creation is waiting for liberation or freedom. How will the creation be liberated? By the power of God. Where is this power of God? In heaven? Yes but that power has also been deposited in the sons of God. Creation is not waiting for God. Creation is waiting for the sons of God to manifest their true self. If you are saved then you are the one your world or creation is waiting to be used of God to set her (creation) free. Whenever God wants to do something in the earth He looks for a man or a woman. When men groan for help and deliverance God will send a man or a woman to bring help and deliverance. When men groan or cry to God, He empowers a man and sends them to bring help. When the earth groans God sends a son or a daughter of God to bring deliverance.

Now therefore, behold, the cry of the children of Israel is come unto me: and I have also seen the oppression wherewith the Egyptians oppress them. Come now therefore, and I will send thee unto Pharaoh, that thou mayest bring forth my people the children of Israel out of Egypt.-Exodus 3:9-10

Israel cried for help and God looked for a man called Moses and sent him to go liberate the children of Israel from bondage and oppression.

And the children of Israel cried unto the LORD: for he had nine hundred chariots of iron; and twenty years he mightily oppressed the children of Israel. And Deborah, a prophetess, the wife of Lapidoth, she judged Israel at that time. - Judges 4:3-4

Again the children of Israel cried. God heard and sent a woman called Deborah to go and liberate the children of Israel from their harsh bondage.

Your world has been groaning to be set free. And now God has sent you to go and liberate your world. This is that time your world has been waiting for. We are living in the days of the manifestation of the **sons of God**. Sons and daughters of the Most High God will arise and be used of God to change lives of the **sons of men**. These sons and daughters of God will be willing, fearless and ready battle axes in the hands of their Father God to liberate the souls of men from the bondage of sin and corruption (disease, death, poverty, failure and all forms of darkness). Sons that will arise and walk in divine authority to reclaim territories and lost souls for God. They will turn the sons of men from the power of Satan to the power of God.

To open their eyes, and to turn them from darkness to light, and from the power of Satan unto God, that they may receive forgiveness of sins, and inheritance among them which are sanctified by faith that is in me.- Act 26:18

The same thing he said to Apostle Paul is what He is saying to you today

But rise, and stand upon thy feet: for I have appeared unto thee for this purpose, to make thee a minister and a witness both of these things which thou hast seen, and of those things in the which I will appear unto thee. Act 26:16

God is not satisfied with you being saved and sitting in the church pews waiting for the rapture or that time you will get to heaven. While you are on earth He wants to use you as His battle axe. This is awesome and what a privilege to be a weapon in the hands of God. If you are a child of God you are His weapon to break in pieces nations and to destroy kingdoms. You are a restorer of hope to men, setting them free, destroying nations and kingdoms oppressing men.

Thou art my battle axe and weapons of war: for with thee will I break in pieces the nations, and with thee will I destroy kingdoms- Jeremiah 51:20

God is looking for willing and available sons and daughters of God who will be used to set their world free. They will set captives free, open blind eyes, cause the lame to walk, rebuild broken down walls and lives. God is enlisting spiritual soldiers of light for this end time push to rescue men and women from sin and corruption. Are you ready and willing to be used of the LORD? If you are then jump in and enlist in God's army. It's time to unleash the sons of God. God has put power, grace and anointing upon the lives of His children and it is not for fun or decoration. It is to liberate men from the bondage of sin and death.

*But ye shall receive **power,** after that the Holy Ghost is come upon you: and ye shall be witnesses unto me both in Jerusalem, and in all Judaea, and in Samaria, and unto the uttermost part of the earth. Act 1:8*

Christ was anointed with power and the Holy Ghost and He went about doing good and setting free the oppressed. He did not sit back and do nothing or sit in church singing praise and worship songs and feeling good with Himself. He went about doing good and setting the captives free.

How God anointed Jesus of Nazareth with the Holy Ghost and with power: who went about doing good, and healing all that were oppressed of the devil; for God was with him. -Act 10:38

Jesus Christ was born a child but He grew, arose and took his place as a son healing the oppressed and doing good by reason of God's power and anointing upon His life. That same anointing is available to every child of God in a measure. If His children will arise and take their place as sons and daughters, He will do even greater miracles than we saw in the first church in the Acts of the Apostles. Remember the glory of the latter shall be greater than that of the former. God is waiting for you to arise and conquer territories for the Kingdom.

The glory of this latter house shall be greater than of the former, saith the LORD of hosts: and in this place will I give peace, saith the LORD of hosts. – Haggai 2:9

4.2 Goldfish have no hiding place

And there came an angel of the LORD, and sat under an oak which was in Ophrah, that pertained unto Joash the Abiezrite: and his son Gideon threshed wheat by the winepress, to hide it from the Midianites. And the angel of the LORD appeared unto him, and said unto him, The LORD is with thee, thou mighty man of valour. - Judges 6:11 -12

The name Gideon means "warrior". What is a warrior doing scared, running and hiding from what should be scared, running and hiding from him? He is a warrior but he is threshing wheat. He is living below God's standard or plan for his life. God made him a warrior but he is running and hiding from the enemy. He is afraid of what is afraid of him. Is that not like so many today? They are sons but are living like slaves. Children of God who have been set free but they are living like captives. Living below their God given potential. A warrior but he is hiding from the Midianites. Winners but they are living like losers.

Gideon was a mighty man of valor (warrior) but he was hiding and running scared. Living below where and what God planned for Him. Like my father in the LORD- Bishop Fred Addo would say- Gideon was threshing wheat when He should have been thrashing Midianites. He doubts himself and even doubts

God. He is living below his true potential. The angel opens his eyes to his true position as a son and a warrior and a winner. He tells him that God is with him. The devil is no match for a mighty warrior and an even mightier God. Gideon asks the angel that if indeed God is for the nation Israel then where are the miracles they heard He did in the days of their fathers.

And Gideon said unto him, Oh my Lord, if the LORD be with us, why then is all this befallen us? And where be all his miracles which our fathers told us of, saying, did not the LORD bring us up from Egypt? But now the LORD hath forsaken us, and delivered us into the hands of the Midianites. - Judges 6:13

God remains the same yesterday, today and forever. God has not lost any of His power or authority and for sure the season of miracles has not ceased. In fact we are in a season of greater miracles, signs and wonders. Sons and daughters of God need to arise and unleash the power of God that is resident on their inside. We have been running and hiding for too long. The enemy has used lies and deception to restrain the sons of God for too long. Goldfish have no hiding place. Can you hide the sun? No you can't. The darkest of darkness cannot stop the sun from shining and we have been told to let our light shine because a city that is set upon a hill cannot be hidden.

Ye are the light of the world. A city that is set on an hill cannot be hid. - Matthew 5:14

Gideon the warrior was making excuses. We have made excuses and restrained ourselves for too long. We have settled in the wilderness called average for years when by faith we could have been walking in the Promised Land called God's best for our lives. We will no longer walk normal or average. We will walk successfully, excellently and supernaturally. We will let our light shine. The angel said to Gideon- go in this might. The light from a candle is still stronger than the strongest of darkness so stop making excuses and go ahead and shine in the kingdom of your Father. Light has no hiding place and you are the light of the world. The world is waiting for you to light them up and set them free. What the world needs is light. The world is in darkness and what it needs now is not criticism or religion. What the world needs is light. You are that light your world needs and you can't stay hidden anymore. So arise and shine.

4.3 It's time to come to our senses

And when he came to himself, he said, How many hired servants of my father's have bread enough and to spare, and I perish with hunger! - Luke 15:17

The prodigal son found himself in the wilderness after he left home unceremoniously and had wasted his father's resources. He found himself in a place called average. He was begging when he should be commanding things. Defeated and dejected when he should be living in victory and celebrated. One day he came to himself and returned home. The day you discover your true self and your inheritance in God is the day you have come to yourself. The time you discover who you are in God is the day your liberation begins. That is the day you stop settling for less of God and you begin to settle for the best of God. It is time to discover yourself and challenge yourself to reach out for God's best for your life. The day the prodigal son came to his senses was the day he stopped settling for crumbs. Kings or sons do not settle for crumbs when the Father has prepared the whole loaf for them. You are settling for half when the Father has prepared the whole for you.

Reminds me of a guy called Mephibosheth. He is royalty but he is living in penury. He is an heir of the kingdom but he is living like a dog. He even called himself a dog. A prince but he is living like a pauper. He lived at Lodebar for many years until the King had mercy on him. I declare that the set time for God's favor has come. The King of kings is set to bring you out from the back and put you in front. He is bringing you out of the wilderness to take you to the Promised Land.

Mephibosheth lived at a place called Lodebar- place of average, mediocrity and reproach. One day the king empowered him and he left that place of shame. The King of kings- Jehovah God is empowering the sons of God to leave their "Lodebar" for their next level. You will not stay at that place anymore for you are moving upward, forward and ahead in Jesus name. You are leaving Lodebar.

And the king said, Is there not yet any of the house of Saul, that I may shew the kindness of God unto him? And Ziba said unto the king, Jonathan hath yet a son, which is lame on his feet. And the king said unto him, Where is he? And Ziba said unto the king, Behold, he is in the house of Machir, the son of Ammiel, in

Lodebar. Then king David sent, and fetched him out of the house of Machir, the son of Ammiel, from Lodebar. Now when Mephibosheth, the son of Jonathan, the son of Saul, was come unto David, he fell on his face, and did reverence. And David said, Mephibosheth. And he answered, Behold thy servant! And David said unto him, Fear not: for I will surely shew thee kindness for Jonathan thy father's sake, and will restore thee all the land of Saul thy father; and thou shalt eat bread at my table continually.

And he bowed himself, and said, What is thy servant, that thou shouldest look upon such a dead dog as I am? Then the king called to Ziba, Saul's servant, and said unto him, I have given unto thy master's son all that pertained to Saul and to all his house. Thou therefore, and thy sons, and thy servants, shall till the land for him, and thou shalt bring in the fruits, that thy master's son may have food to eat: but Mephibosheth thy master's son shall eat bread alway at my table. Now Ziba had fifteen sons and twenty servants. 2Samuel 9:3-10

God's plan is to use you and me to invade the natural with the supernatural. It's time to arise and make your Father God proud. We are living in the days of His power. It's time to unleash the sons of God. We are like lions that have been caged, restrained and put on a leash. It's time to unleash the sons of God for the benefit of creation and to bring glory to God. God is not glorified when children, men and women are dying prematurely of sickness and disease. He is not happy that children and nations are starving to death. The world needs help and the sons and daughters of the kingdom of light are the ones God will use as channels or instruments to bring help to a needy world.

It's your season for restoration and reclaiming all your kingdom rights and privileges. It's time for the sons of God to manifest in the earth. The enemy has stolen enough territory from us. We have been blinded by religion and so the enemy has stolen our inheritance as sons and daughters of the kingdom. Christ died and paid for my portion and your portion in life. I don't know about you but I am taking what belongs to me. I challenge you to take yours for your inheritance in God is there for the taking. I can't take it for you because I am busy taking mine. Nobody can take it for you because hopefully they should be busy possessing theirs if they are a son or a daughter of God.

This is the season for sons and daughters to awake to their kingdom rights, privileges and responsibilities. I challenge you not to settle for less than the best of God. Don't stop at good if you can get better. Don't stay at better when you can reach best. Don't settle for best when God has prepared excellent for you. Why pitch your tent in excellent when you can build a mansion at the place called greatness. Don't settle at having a good home when God wants you to have a great home. Don't stay running when God has given you wings to fly. Why do you want to be satisfied with living like a chicken when God wants you to be an eagle? No more will sons live like slaves and slaves live like sons. God must be tired that sons are on foot and slaves are riding on horseback. That evil is set to be corrected.

We have been delivered from sin and slavery to sin. We have a choice now. The devil and the world have lied to us that we do not have a choice. But God said we have a choice. We can choose life instead of death. We can choose blessing or curses. It's our choice to make. Let's stop being deceived. God does not force His will on any human. If He did, Eve would not have lost her Eden. If God forced his will on us all men would be going to heaven. Choose blessing. Choose right and you will experience right. Choices affect what we get in life so determine to choose right.

I call heaven and earth to record this day against you, that I have set before you life and death, blessing and cursing: therefore choose life, that both thou and thy seed may live- Deuteronomy 30:19

Sin is no longer your master. The devil has been defeated and the power of sin has been broken. We have been translated out of the kingdom of darkness into the kingdom of light. We are sons and daughters of the Most High God. But to experience sonship we need to take our proper positions. Everyone that is born into God's kingdom is a child but we are not born as sons and daughters. To possess your inheritance you must grow into a son or a daughter. It is when we grow into sons that we can possess our inheritance and help others to possess their inheritance. God delivers or saves us from sin so that we can become deliverers or saviors. He delivers us so we can be used to deliver others. We are blessed to be a blessing and saved to save others. We are healed to heal others and reached so that we can reach others with the love and power of God.

Sons and daughters of God! It is time to arise and shine. It's time for darkness to come to the light and be delivered. It's time that the people who are walking in darkness will see the great light that is God in us shine through us. We will no longer live in fear, being deceived by the devil, running and hiding. We will no longer fear because the enemy has been defeated and dethroned. He has been dethroned and the greater one lives in us by the Spirit of God. We are kingdom warriors destined to win and we will arise and take our position in these last days before the coming of the LORD to set the captives free.

The earth has been waiting for the manifestation of the sons of God and that time of manifestation is now. It is time for the kingdom of light to unleash the sons and daughters of God. It is time to unleash the sons and daughters of God on the world

4.4 Unleash the sons

Oh that will be a day! A day for rebuilding your city, a day for stretching your arms, spreading your wings! – Micah 7:11 MSG

I once read the story of how elephants are trained by their trainers in a circus. It is said that the hind leg of a baby elephant is held with a chain (leash) which in turn is tied to a metal stake or peg in the ground. The elephant tries to go forward but it cannot because of the leash tied to its leg. Try as it may it can't get free and as it struggles to break free and move forward it even wounds itself drawing pain and blood. After many failed attempts it gives up. As the elephant grows older, off cause it gets bigger. The trainer even replaces the metal peg or hook which is used to fasten the chain to the ground with a wooden one. At this point you would expect that this older, bigger and more experienced elephant has more than enough strength to pull the peg out of the ground and run free. However it has long ceased attempting to pull free. Many failed attempts at trying to be free and even the pain it felt attempting to be free have caused the elephant to cease trying to break free and move forward.

The elephant has become conditioned by past failure and so will not take the steps needed to pull or push forward.

Humans are so much like the elephant. We are tied down even restricted by our past failed attempts and failures. We are making excuses why we can't fly. In John 5, Jesus asked the man by the pool of Bethesda- will you be made whole and he answered and said I have no man to help me. Whenever I want to enter someone else enters before me you hear him say. God called Moses to go lead the children of Israel out of Egypt. Moses starts to give reasons why he is not the best man for the job.

Look at Gideon the warrior. Gideon the winner. A fearful and intimidated warrior. A warrior living in fear and doubt. Warrior indeed. He said- I am the least in my father's house. My father's house is the smallest in the clan. My clan is the smallest clan in the tribe of Israel. Among the tribes I am the least. Negative, negative, negative. I can't, I can't, and I can't. Not good enough, not good enough, not good enough. Not capable, not capable, not capable.

Held down, limited, held back, caged, hampered and stopped. That has been the story of many children of the Most High God. All that is set to change because God is set to unleash the sons of God. The world will not have to wait any longer for the manifestation of the sons of God. What does the term "unleash" mean? It means to turn loose. It means to free someone or something from restraint. The things that have stopped you from exercising your sonship rights will stop you no more because we have entered the days and seasons for the manifestation of the sons of God.

Matthew 21:2-3 tells us the account of a certain donkey.

Saying unto them, Go into the village over against you, and straightway ye shall find an ass tied, and a colt with her: loose them, and bring them unto me. And if any man say ought unto you, ye shall say, The Lord hath need of them; and straightway he will send them.

The Master had need of it but it was tied down. What did Christ say? Go loose the donkey and bring it to me. Come to Christ with all your weaknesses, liabilities, sin, inabilities and even abilities. Come as you are. He can and will use you if you will come. The time has come to loose and unleash the sons and daughters of God. You have been held down too long. God needs you. Your world needs you. You are alive for a reason and for a season. We are all created to make a difference in the earth. We are created by God to solve a problem or problems in the earth. God created Adam because He needed someone to tend the earth and there was no one until He found Adam. Adam was blessed by God and he (Adam) was a blessing to his world.

God by His spirit and power is unleashing the sons of God in these last days. You are blessed but it is time to be a blessing. God is raising sons to overthrow kingdoms and every high thing that exalts itself against the knowledge of God. He is raising sons. Sons that will tear off every leash of fear, limitation and excuse that has held the church down over the years. Are you ready? If you are, God is ready. Remember you are His battle axe. You can't swing an unwilling or unavailable battle axe. No surprise that Psalm 110:3 AMP says-

Thy people shall be willing in the day of thy power, in the beauties of holiness from the womb of the morning: thou hast the dew of thy youth.

God has always been ready and waiting for the children to arise and take their place as sons and exercise their authority as sons. The baby "elephants" will no longer remain babies in the LORD. They will grow into adulthood (sons, daughters and even fathers) and tear every stake that has held them down. They will grow into sons and with God on their inside they will triumph over the works of darkness setting men free, healing the sick, casting out demons and raising the dead.

I write unto you, little children, because your sins are forgiven you for his name's sake. I write unto you, fathers, because ye have known him that is from the beginning. I write unto you, young men, because ye have overcome the wicked one. I write unto you, little children, because ye have known the Father. I have written unto you, fathers, because ye have known him that is from the beginning. I have written unto you, young men, because ye are strong, and the word of God abideth in you, and ye have overcome the wicked one. -1John 2:12-14

God's desire has always been for children to grow into sons and from sons to fathers. As they do they will enter new levels of power and authority and conquer more territory for their Father God while affecting their world positively for God. He called His disciples to himself and gave them power and authority to heal the sick, raise the dead and cast out devils. That calling or instruction is still ours to execute even now.

Heal the sick, cleanse the lepers, raise the dead, cast out devils: freely ye have received, freely give- Matthew 10:8

We have entered the days of the manifestation of the sons of God. We are pulling out every "peg" and tearing every leash that has held us down. No prison will be able to hold us down any longer. The prison doors were not able to hold Paul and Silas down- *Acts 16*. The gates of their prison door were pulled up at the hinges and all. We will not be held down any longer. The chains on their feet were loosed. Every chain or leash holding you down is broken right now in Jesus name. Gideon broke free and God unleashed him on the Midianites that were tormenting God's people and he went from victory to victory.

Concerning Isaac the word of God had this to say

And the man waxed great, and went forward, and grew until he became very great- Genesis 26:13.

This is your story child of God. You belong in the lineage of Isaac. He went forward until he achieved greatness. You too can achieve greatness if you so desire. It's the same God Isaac had that you have. It's time to remove every leash that has held you down. You are not limited by your environment. You are limited by your faith. If your faith says yes God will reward you with a miracle. If your faith says you can then God will supply the strength and you will.

You are a son or daughter of a great God. You can achieve greatness. Don't stop till you reach greatness. Let nothing stop you until you reach greatness. Remove every leash you and life have placed on you. Go ahead and spread your wings and fly. You are set to be unleashed for the benefit of your world and to the glory of God. It is time to unleash the sons and daughters of God.

ABILITY

5

POWER AND AUTHORITY
TO UNLEASH GREATNESS

Divine power plays with human affairs. - Ovid

This is the word of the LORD to Zerubbabel: You will not succeed by your own strength or by your own power, but by my Spirit, says the LORD All-powerful-Zechariah 4:6 NCV.

There is natural power and there is supernatural power. What you might call natural ability and supernatural ability. Success and greatness is possible yet you cannot unleash success and greatness without power. You will succeed if you will but you will not succeed by your own strength or power. No matter your skill, qualification, natural ability, experience and exposure you cannot make it with your own natural strength alone. The prophet Zechariah said so and it is so even in our day today.

Gideon succeeded because there was an extra dimension called supernatural ability that was bestowed on him by God. God gave him supernatural ability and that made a difference in his life. Let's look at this supernatural ability that was operating in the life of Gideon.

5.1 The LORD is with you

The angel announced to Gideon- the LORD is with you. Fear disappeared when he heard that the LORD is with him. The maker of heaven and earth is with him. That makes a whole lot of difference. At this point in time Israel had gone through much trouble, frustration and discouragement. They continued to suffer in the hands of Midianites for seven years. Gideon found it difficult to believe that God is still with Israel but He was still with them. After all God has declared that He will never leave nor forsake Israel.

When God is with you fear should have no place

And there came an angel of the LORD, and sat under an oak which was in Ophrah, that pertained unto Joash the Abiezrite: and his son Gideon threshed wheat by the winepress, to hide it from the Midianites. - Judges 6:11

Fear is an enemy and it has torment. Fear limits a man. We see a warrior but he is limited by fear. Fear does not come from God. It is fear that keeps you from taking steps towards being what and whom God wants you to be. Fear kept Gideon from unleashing the winner in him. Afraid of whom and what should be afraid of him. Fear kept him from moving forward towards success and greatness. It's been said that the fear of failure is worse than failure itself. Fear keeps a winner down and the word of God says that we are more than conquerors or winners through Christ who loved us

Nay, in all these things we are more than conquerors through him that loved us. - Romans 8:37

After the angel spoke the word of God to him fear melted. The word of God is light and light will always dispel darkness. The angel said to Gideon- the LORD is with you.

And the angel of the LORD appeared unto him, and said unto him, The LORD is with thee, thou mighty man of valour. – Judges 6:12

You do not have to fear when the LORD of the whole universe is with you. We are living in dangerous or perilous times and because of fear the hearts of men will fail and are failing them.

Men's hearts failing them for fear, and for looking after those things which are coming on the earth: for the powers of heaven shall be shaken. – Luke 21:26

It has been stated that the phrase "fear not" appears more than 365 times in the bible. That means if you like you have at least one "fear not" for each day in a calendar year. Let us list some of those "fear nots" in scripture for our encouragement and motivation.

Christ said fear not because His love and care for you is total and guaranteed

But even the very hairs of your head are all numbered. Fear not therefore: ye are of more value than many sparrows. – Luke 12:7

Fear not for what you need to make life meaningful and to live the abundant life has already prepared for you by your Father God. Fear not because it is your Father's pleasure to give you the kingdom.

Fear not, little flock; for it is your Father's good pleasure to give you the kingdom. - Luke 12:32

Fear not for He that promised you will not fail. What He has promised to do He will do. He is coming with what you need

Fear not, daughter of Sion: behold, thy King cometh, sitting on an ass's colt. - John 12:15

Fear not because you are valuable and precious in the sight of God. He redeemed you to himself. That makes you very special so fear not

Fear ye not therefore, ye are of more value than many sparrows.-Matthew 10:31

Fear will stop you. Fear will immobilize you and keep you from reaching where God wants you to reach. Fear kept Gideon from unleashing the warrior in him. Fear limited him. To unleash the best of God out of him God first had to help him deal with his fear. God is with you so fear not. Fear not and trust God to become all He wants you to become and to do all He wants you to do.

When God is with you the impossible is possible

But Jesus beheld them, and said unto them, with men this is impossible; but with God all things are possible. –Matthew 19:26

With God all things are possible. When God is with you nothing shall be impossible for you. Nothing is impossible for the creator God. He is LORD and nothing is hard for Him. What is the thing fighting you? It looks impossible but it is possible with God. Nothing shall be impossible for God and for the believer in God who believes it. All things are possible said Christ.

Jesus said unto him, if thou canst believe, all things are possible to him that believeth. - Mark 9:23.

If you will believe all things are possible with you. God has no problem believing this. The problem is always with man not God. As far as God is concerned all things are possible for God. Man on the other hand needs to believe all things are possible to be able to achieve the impossible. The impossible is possible for God and for the believer who believes that the impossible is possible.

Gideon needed to have his mind renewed. He believed that the Midianites were a tall opposition and impossible to handle. The angel showed him that God is with him and that because God is with him the imposing and intimidating Midianite army is not impossible to be defeated. The problem is never with God rather the problem is with our believing. The problem is not God's ability rather the problem is our thinking. We become what we think.

For as he thinketh in his heart, so is he: Eat and drink, saith he to thee; but his heart is not with thee. – Proverbs 23:7

The Israelite army led by Saul saw Goliath as impossible to handle but David saw Goliath as possible to handle. What is the difference? Their perspective or thinking is what is different. Two people in similar situation can get different outcomes even when they have the same God. Why? If they think differently they will get different results. One person thinks or believes that for this sickness there is no way out. The other thinks and believes that God will make a way. Remember it shall be to you according to your faith.

Then touched he their eyes, saying, According to your faith be it unto you.-Matthew 9:29

God will go as far as your faith can go. You will certainly go as far as your faith can go. If you say and believe that it is possible for you to be healed you will be healed. Doctors can say to you that it is impossible for you to get healed. That is their belief but ultimately what matters the most is what you believe. Your faith is more important than our faith or their faith. What is your faith saying? Remember that it shall be to you according to your faith and not according to our faith.

Who hath believed our report? And to whom is the arm of the LORD revealed? – Isaiah 53:1

Believing in the power of God connects you to the power (arm) of God. The power of God is what you need to accomplish the impossible. Raise your faith to God and He will unleash His power in that situation of yours. Change needs power to happen but for power to be revealed in that situation God requires only your faith. Surely that can't be too much to give.

An angel appeared to a young girl and gave her a message that she would have a son. She does not have a husband and is not married so how will she possibly give birth to a child. The angel tells her nothing is impossible for God.

For with God nothing shall be impossible. And Mary said, Behold the handmaid of the Lord; be it unto me according to thy word. And the angel departed from her. – Luke 1:37-38

The angel says with God nothing shall be impossible. Mary just agrees with the angel's prophecy even though she does not know how it will happen. Let it be unto me (not us) according to thy word. What has God spoken concerning you? It looks impossible but it is possible if you can only believe it is possible. Agree with God and He will reward your faith with a miracle because the impossible is possible for God and for the one that believes that the impossible is possible.

When God is with you miracles are sure

There was a man of the Pharisees, named Nicodemus, a ruler of the Jews. The same came to Jesus by night, and said unto him, Rabbi, we know that thou art a teacher come from God: for no man can do these miracles that thou doest, except God be with him. – John 3:1-2

The Pharisees were one of the biggest critics of Jesus' life and ministry. Very often they were wrong in their opinions but at least this once one of them (Nicodemus) got it right. He said no man can do miracles except God is with him. He was absolutely correct. When you are connected to Jesus you are connected to the source of miracles. When you are connected to the God of signs and wonders you will be a sign and a wonder and you can do signs and wonders. The God of miracles will do miracles with you and through you in the life of others.

He that believeth and is baptized shall be saved; but he that believeth not shall be damned. And these signs shall follow them that believe. In my name shall they cast out devils; they shall speak with new tongues. They shall take up serpents; and if they drink any deadly thing, it shall not hurt them; they shall lay hands on the sick, and they shall recover. - Mark 16:16-18

Signs are to follow the believer in Christ. You will no longer be a sign-less believer. It is an error for a believer to be following signs and wonders. Believers are to command signs and wonders. Believers are not supposed to follow miracles. Miracles are to follow believers. Believers are following miracles, signs and wonders today because we do not know the ways of God. Too many baby Christians who have not grown into their status as sons and daughters. Moses commanded signs and wonders because he was a son.

Gideon was looking for miracles when miracles should be pursuing him. The supernatural ought to be natural for children of God. The supernatural ought to be normal for the believer in Christ. Signs follow believers in Christ and because you are a believer signs should follow you. You won't be a sigh instead you will be a sign. You will not look for miracles rather you will command miracles. Listen to what Gideon said

And Gideon said unto him, Oh my Lord, if the LORD be with us, why then is all this befallen us? And where be all his miracles which our fathers told us of, saying, did not the LORD bring us up from Egypt? But now the LORD hath forsaken us, and delivered us into the hands of the Midianites. – Judges 6:13 KJV

Gideon had lived a mundane or ordinary life until God commissioned him to go fight the Midianites. It was no fault of God rather it was Gideon's fault that his life lacked signs and wonders. You have wondered at the wonders happening in the life of others but now it is time to be a wonder. There is a realm of signs and wonders that God will have every child of God to operate or living in. Gideon had been a sigh not a sign for too long. However things were about to change. He had been exploited for too long when he should have been doing exploits.

Gideon's life was about to change because for the first time he understood that God is with him and believed it too. For the first time he understood that if God is with me, my life cannot be devoid or empty of miracles. You ought to walk in the miraculous because God is with you. Living miraculously is usual for the believer in Christ because the God who does miracles is with him. Don't settle for an ordinary life lacking miracles. Settle for the supernatural and experience a continual life of miracles because God is with you.

When God is with you the odds are in your favour

There will be opposition, obstacles and difficulty in life. Gideon believed that if God is with him then he should not have opposition. There will come opposition to your position some times. That is why you need God to be on your side. When God is on your side the opposition no matter how big cannot be bigger than the God who is with you. No wonder the psalmist says

The LORD is my light and my salvation; whom shall I fear? the LORD is the strength of my life; of whom shall I be afraid? When the wicked, even mine enemies and my foes, came upon me to eat up my flesh, they stumbled and fell. Though an host should encamp against me, my heart shall not fear: though war should rise against me, in this will I be confident.- Psalm 27:1-3

See how many times he mentions the name of the LORD. Yes the enemies are there. Yes the wicked are opposing him. Yes there are foes and a host of trouble makers and trouble. Sometimes when trouble comes it comes as a host (many or multitude). In the midst of all this he says my heart shall not fear. He said the LORD is the strength of my (his) life and so he will not fear. The LORD is more than enough for all your, foes, opposition and host or legion of troubles. Your God is more than enough. He can handle anything.

Yes the God of the universe can handle anything and nothing is too hard for him. Gideon was about to learn this truth because God spoke to him and said

But if thou fear to go down, go thou with Phurah thy servant down to the host. And thou shalt hear what they say; and afterward shall thine hands be strengthened

to go down unto the host. Then went he down with Phurah his servant unto the outside of the armed men that were in the host. – Judges 7:10-11 KJV

The enemy that he was afraid of was afraid of him. Knowledge or understanding that God is with you strengthened Gideon's hand. Where there was fear before there was now faith. When God is with you the odds are not against you rather they are in your favor. When God is with you the size of the opposition is irrelevant. Tall as the opposition maybe it can't be taller or mightier than God. Again hear what the word of God says in Romans 8

What shall we then say to these things? If God be for us, who can be against us? – Romans 8:31

If God is for you who can be against you. If God is with you then sickness and disease cannot beat you. You and God are unbeatable. You and God are not disadvantaged. The odds are definitely in your favor if God is with you. God and you are a formidable foe for any foe. So do not fear the taunts of the wicked. Don't be intimidated by the opposition. They are too small for your God. Goliath is no match for David and his God. David knew so and he affirmed so. God did the rest.

And I went out after him, and smote him, and delivered it out of his mouth: and when he arose against me, I caught him by his beard, and smote him, and slew him. Thy servant slew both the lion and the bear: and this uncircumcised Philistine shall be as one of them, seeing he hath defied the armies of the living God. – 1 Samuel 17:35-37.

Fear not for God is with you. The opposition looks big but it is not bigger than God. You have a very significant edge in life when you have God with you. God in your life makes a very big difference. No matter where you have been or what you have been through you can still unleash the hidden potential inside you. God on your side gives you the edge or advantage you need to be all that God wants you to become and to do all that He wants you to do.

When the LORD is with you success is guaranteed.

There shall not any man be able to stand before thee all the days of thy life: as I was with Moses, so I will be with thee: I will not fail thee, nor forsake thee. - Joshua 1:5

Success is not guaranteed if the LORD is not with you. God with you means you have too much on your side to fail. Gideon among his many fears was afraid to fail. He even saw himself as a failure because he said to the angel if God is with us why are we passing through what we are passing through. God with you does not mean you will get it right the first or even the second, third or sixth time. It means that no matter how many times you fall you will still succeed if you don't stop trying for success. The righteous fall seven times but they rise again.

For a just man falleth seven times, and riseth up again: but the wicked shall fall into mischief. – Proverbs 24:16

One Japanese proverb says- "Fall seven times, stand up eight times". Failure happens when you fall down and refuse to get up. You are not a failure until you refuse to rise up after you have fallen. A knock down they say is not a knock out. You will succeed because the LORD is with you. Don't be afraid to try out for success because the LORD is with you. Joshua looked at the enormous task to lead a very stubborn nation into the Promised Land. He had been assistant to Moses during Moses' ministry and he had seen all that the children of Israel had put the man of God through. Who would not be afraid? God assures him just as He assured Joshua with words by saying thus:

There shall not any man be able to stand before thee all the days of thy life: as I was with Moses, so I will be with thee: I will not fail thee, nor forsake thee. - Joshua 1:5

You are afraid to fail but I decree that you will not fail because God is with you. He is your senior partner and does not have a history of failure. Don't be afraid to enter that marriage relationship He has shown you because He is with you. He will not fail you and your marriage will not fail. Pursue the dream He gave you for He is with you and will not fail you. With God on your side you cannot and will not fail. All your dreams are possible. Success is possible because God is with you. Gideon succeeded because God is with him. You have the same God that Gideon had and you will succeed. You will unleash the winner in you. The warrior in you will not remain buried. It's time to release the giant in you because God is with you.

Adam was successful as long as he lived in the presence of God. Elijah acknowledged that the God in whose presence he dwells habitual will give him success when he prays.

Elijah the foreigner, who was an alien resident from Gilead, told Ahab, "As the LORD God of Israel lives, in whose presence I'm standing, there will be neither dew nor rain these next several years, except when I say so." – 1 Kings17:1 ISV

Concerning Joseph it was said that the LORD was with him and made him prosper wherever he went.

The LORD was with Joseph and made him successful. He lived in the house of his Egyptian master. – Genesis 39:2 GNB

The presence of God makes the difference in the lives of men. Without the presence of God in your life you will live a less than abundant life. With God you can and should live the abundant life He has designed for you. The presence of God **ALWAYS** makes a difference. The angel said to Mary the LORD is with you. The angel of God said to Gideon- the LORD is with you. God has deposited seeds of greatness inside you so you can't or are not supposed to die unsuccessful and average. You are destined for success and greatness because God is with you.

5.2 God has given you "Doonamis"- the supernatural power of God

The great need of the world today is the spiritual power necessary for the overthrow of evil, for the establishment of righteousness and for the ushering in of the era of perpetual peace and that spiritual power begins in the surrender of the individual to God. It commences with obedience to the first commandment. - William Jennings Bryan

There are two realms or worlds- the unseen but very real spirit world or realm and the seen or visible physical world. Spiritual power is of two kinds too. There is the power of darkness and there is the power of light. The power of darkness is stronger than physical power but it (power of darkness) still has limitations. The power of light is the power of God. It is the highest and greatest power available and it is unlimited. All power belongs to God. He however has allocated some power to the kingdom of darkness. The power of darkness is that limited power that devils and their agents wield or exercise.

Jesus said, "I saw Satan fall like lightning from heaven. Listen, I have given you power to walk on snakes and scorpions, power that is greater than the enemy has. So nothing will hurt you. But you should not be happy because the spirits obey you but because your names are written in heaven." - Luke 10:18-20 NCV.

Christ means what He says and He says what He means. He said to the disciples - I give you power and that this power is greater than anything that the enemy has. Who said the enemy does not have power. You probably don't know the bible. Some believe he- the devil does not have power. That's an extreme you must avoid. Others believe he has too much power and that he rules the earth. That is also an extreme belief that you should avoid. Both these extremes are not good for you. Satan and the host of darkness have spiritual power but it is limited power. There is power that is greater than the power of darkness. It is called the power of God or in the Greek d*oonamis.*

The kingdom of darkness has power. If Christ said so then it is so. Don't be deceived. Some believe there is no devil. That is extreme and quite foolish thinking. Satan was a top angel in heaven until he sinned and got kicked out of heaven. And if you know anything about angels the word of God tells us that they excel in strength.

Bless the LORD, ye his angels, that excel in strength, that do his commandments, hearkening unto the voice of his word.- Psalms 103:20

God created angels and he gave them power. Satan was one of such created angels. He was created Lucifer. God gave him power or might like he gave the other angels. Angels are spirit beings who have been empowered by God. Angels have power. That is why we see one angel go out and singlehandedly kill 185000 soldiers.

And it all came to pass, for that night the Angel of the Lord went forth and slew 185,000 in the camp of the Assyrians; and when [the living] arose early in the morning, behold, all these were dead bodies. - 2 Kings 19:35 AMP.

It takes power for one single angel to slay 185,000 soldiers. The angel did so without help from anyone or another angel. Who said angels don't have power. They do. Satan is an angel. Right now he is a fallen angel. That means as an angel who had not yet fallen man was higher in spiritual rank than him. Even now that he is a fallen angel redeemed man has authority over him. That should give you confidence that he- Satan can't "beat" you except you let him.

Angels have power and Satan though a fallen angel still has power. The Angels that rebelled with him also have some power. The power of darkness is real. The host of darkness has power. But it is limited power. Power that can fail and has limits.

There is power that is greater than all other power be it physical or spiritual. And it is the power of God. Christ is LORD over the universe and is the source of all power. All other creatures depend on Christ to give them power. The power of God is more real than any other power. It is unlimited power. Greek translation of the word power in the New Testament is *doonamis*. Doonamis is the power of God. It is the best, the greatest power that is available in heaven, on earth or in hell. No greater power than Doonamis- the power of God. All other power is subject to Doonamis or the power of God. That is reason for faith and joy for if you are a child of God power- Doonamis is on your side.

THEN JESUS called together the Twelve [apostles] and gave them power and authority over all demons, and to cure diseases- Luke 9:1AMP

Christ called His disciples and gave them the very power of God- Doonamis. The unlimited power of God has been given to you by God. If you are a disciple of Christ you have Doonamis or the power of God with you. The power of God is real. Satan is not bigger or higher than God. He is created. And the created cannot be bigger or higher than the creator. He has power but your God is the source of power. Satan and darkness have power but God is the source of power. The channel cannot be bigger or stronger than its source. Satan is like a lion but Christ is the Lion of the tribe of Judah. Satan and his legion of demons have delegated power but God has all power. Satan because he is an angel has little power but God has all power.

Satan has might but God is almighty. Your God is all mighty. With the might that he (Satan) has his might or power has limitations. The power of darkness is limited but the power of light is unlimited. Remember how the rod of Aaron swallowed the rod of the magicians.

For they cast down every man his rod, and they became serpents: but Aaron's rod swallowed up their rods. – Exodus 7:12

Where the power of evil got tired and failed the power of God just began. Darkness uses evil power to work magic; spells, evil and wickedness. Light uses Doonamis to work miracles. Magic will fail but miracles from God are forever. God gave the disciples doonamis- the unlimited power of God. You have the power of God inside you. You are filled with doonamis. If you have Christ you are filled with doonamis or the power of God. And if you don't have Christ you don't have this doonamis. You are vulnerable if you don't have Christ. If you don't have Christ you don't have Doonamis power and so are vulnerable to the power of darkness.

Just before Christ ascended to heaven he gave the 12 apostles a command. He said tarry you in Jerusalem until you are endued- clothed with power from on high.

And behold, I will send forth upon you what My Father has promised; but remain in the city [Jerusalem] until you are clothed with power from on high. - Luke 24:49AMP

Simply beautiful. He said they would be clothed with power or doonamis. Are you a disciple of Christ? God wants to clothe you with power from on high. It's not demonic power. It's power from on high. The very power of God. It's doonamis. The miracle working power of God. God wants to clothe you with the supernatural, unlimited, unstoppable power of God. You can wear this doonamis the way humans wear clothing. God desires you to be soaked in doonamis. The world is looking for power. That's why men go to any length to get spiritual power. The spiritual power that men search for, give anything and do anything to get is what God has given us freely and it is better, higher and greater.

Heal the sick, cleanse the lepers, raise the dead, cast out devils: freely ye have received, freely give. – Matthew 10:8

He gave the disciples spiritual power or doonamis. If you are His child you have received doonamis or the very power of God.

What comes next is very important: I am sending what my Father promised to you, so stay here in the city until he arrives, until you're equipped with power from on high." Luke 24:49 MSG

In the message translation He said- what comes next is very important. Very important for your success, achievement and greatness in life. Very important if you must unleash the success and greatness that God has planted inside you. There is a warrior in you but you need power to unleash the warrior in you. Without this doonamis or the power of God you will live life exploited when you should be doing exploits. You will live life a victim instead of a victor. You will live life threshed, thrashed and thumped by darkness. Gideon lived life below his true status of warrior because he did not know he had been given spiritual might or power to live as a warrior. He is a warrior but he is threshing wheat. He was threshed, thrashed and thumped by darkness until God opened his eyes to see that he (Gideon) had the unlimited power of God with him. Power was with him and in him but he was living like one with no power. Doonamis or the power of God empowers you to live a supernatural, abundant and overcoming life. You don't have to live life down, defeated, desperate and frustrated. There is power on your side. The power of God empowers you to live a signs and wonders filled life. The wonder working power of God empowers you to live a wonders full and a wonderful life. God planned for you to live the abundant life and you will if you will tap into the power that He has made available to you. This power or *doonamis* will make you outstanding and cause you to standout.

Ye are the light of the world. A city that is set on an hill cannot be hid. – Matthew 5:14

Christ said to them- stay here till He arrives. Who was He talking about? He was talking about the Holy Spirit of God. With the Holy Ghost comes power-*doonamis*. This power helps you unleash success, signs, wonders and helps you achieve greatness. When the Holy Spirit comes upon them they would be equipped with the power of the Most High God. When the Holy Ghost comes on them (the disciples) they will be equipped with *doonamis*. The Holy Ghost is the *doonamis* (power) of God.

When you are clothed (anointed) with the Holy Ghost you receive the power of God. Doonamis or the power of God rests on you when the Holy Ghost comes upon you. A life of signs, wonders, success, and greatness is guaranteed when you have doonamis. With the power of God you can reach heights that you would never have reached without this power or doonamis of God. The Doonamis of God empowers you for a life of signs, wonders, success and greatness. This *doonamis* turned ordinary unschooled fishermen to extraordinary men who turned their world around. It is this *doonamis* (power) of God that will unleash success, greatness, dominion out of you. You can't stay down when the *doonamis* of God is operating in your life. Everyone who receives this *doonamis* cannot remain beaten rather they are turned to world beaters and achievers. John the Baptist had this *doonamis* or power of God

And he will go on before the Lord, in the spirit and power of Elijah, to turn the hearts of the parents to their children and the disobedient to the wisdom of the righteous—to make ready a people prepared for the Lord." - Luke 1:17 NIV.

There was a spirit that was upon the life of Elijah. The spirit of God was upon Elijah. The spirit of God is a spirit of power. The angel prophesied that the spirit and power upon the life of Elijah would rest upon John. He was filled with this power or *doonamis* from his mother's womb. John was filled with *doonamis* from his mother's womb. John succeeded in ministry and became great because the *doonamis* of God was upon his life. God wants to clothe you with power or *doonamis*. When you received the Holy Ghost you became clothed with the *doonamis* of God. If you have not received the Holy Ghost evidenced by speaking in tongues you have not yet received the fullness of this *doonamis* of God.

To fulfill his earthly ministry even Christ had to be clothed with this *doonamis*. He walked the earth as flesh and blood. He did not walk this earth as God. He walked this earth as a man that was endued or clothed with the *doonamis* of God. When the Holy Ghost came upon Him, He was filled with doonamis or the power of God.

And the Holy Spirit came down on him in the form of a dove. Then a voice came from heaven, saying, "You are my Son, whom I love, and I am very pleased with you." When Jesus began his ministry, he was about thirty years old. People thought that Jesus was Joseph's son. Joseph was the son of Heli. - Luke 3:22-23 NCV

His ministry did not kick off until He was baptized with power after the Holy Ghost came upon him. He lived as an obscure carpenter known only within his little village until he was baptized with the Holy Ghost and clothed with power. He did not unleash his ministry in the earth until He received *doonamis*. Success and greatness did not begin for him until he received power. He received *doonamis* and He started His ministry of power, signs, wonders and greatness. God was about to unleash His son in the world but first He - the son (Christ) had to be empowered with *doonamis*. After the Holy Ghost came upon him He received *doonamis* and His ministry jump started. God is set to unleash you on your world. He will baptize you with *doonamis* again and again and again. As Jesus prayed while he was baptized in water the Holy Ghost descended mightily upon Him. If you have not received the Holy Ghost I pray for you today that He will descend upon you and as a result you will be filled with *doonamis* - which is the unlimited, unrestricted and unhindered power of God. *Doonamis* is the unstoppable, unquenchable, unbeatable power of God and it is available for all who will come and submit to God.

And so after He had completed His ministry He gave command to His disciples that they should tarry till they received the Holy Ghost. They were about to kick start their own ministry but they needed *doonamis*. The Holy Ghost would empower them with *doonamis* so He (Christ) told them to wait and they would receive the Holy Ghost. With the Holy Ghost comes *doonamis*. When you receive the Holy Ghost *doonamis* comes upon you. And boy did He descend upon them and transform their ministry and lives.

But when the Holy Spirit comes to you, you will receive power. You will be my witnesses—in Jerusalem, in all of Judea, in Samaria, and in every part of the world. - Acts 1:8 NCV.

Christ said- When the Holy Spirit comes upon you, you will receive power and you will be my witnesses. Effective witnessing for Christ is impossible without the power of God or *doonamis*. Ministry without *doonamis* is misery. Today receive the Holy Ghost in Jesus name. Amen. You have received Christ but you have not received the Holy Ghost. Today I pray for you that you will receive the free gift of the Holy Ghost. With Him comes power or *doonamis*. You have been clothed with the *doonamis* power of God. Unleash success and greatness from within you. There is a warrior inside you. With the *doonamis* you have received you have the ability to unleash the winner inside you. You have received *doonamis* to unleash healing, deliverance and freedom to a world that is still held bound by the power of darkness.

When Gideon understood that he had the power of God to fight the Midianites of mediocrity, barrenness, failure, sickness and disease he stepped out in power and conquered them. He was used of God to deliver the people of God from the oppression of the Midianites. God is looking for vessels to invest His *doonamis* power. Every investor looks for returns or yield on their investment. God has invested power in your life. What are you doing with the power that He has put inside you? It's time to come out from threshing wheat and live like the warrior or winner God created you to be. There is a warrior or winner inside you- the true you is a winner and is still hidden. It's time to unleash the warrior in you for you have the power or Doonamis to do just that. And you will.

5.3 God has also given you "Exousia"- spiritual authority

THEN JESUS called together the twelve [apostles] and gave them power and authority over all demons, and to cure diseases, - Luke 9:1AMP

Just like there is natural power and there is spiritual power there is also natural authority and there is spiritual authority. Examples of natural authority include the traffic policeman who has been given authority by the state to control traffic on the streets. Or the tax man who has government given authority to collect taxes. The authority the governor or president exercises over a state or nation is also natural authority. The headmaster who administers the affairs of the primary school is walking in natural authority. All of these persons have been given authority by the laws of the land to exercise their authority.

Authority has been defined as delegated influence or control. It can also be defined as the right to exercise power. The right to demand something and it gets done. The traffic warden has authority to tell you to stop your car when you get to the traffic junction. The taxman has right to demand for your taxes. The government of the land has empowered him to demand and receive your taxes.

Far more important and more powerful than natural authority is spiritual authority. It's unseen but it is more real. In the beginning when God created man he gave him authority (right) to rule and dominate the earth. We see Adam exercising that authority because whatever name he gave to the animals in the garden that was the name that stood. Even God did not reverse or change the name because He had already delegated spiritual authority to Adam. When Adam sinned however he transferred that authority to Satan. Its little wonder that we hear Satan declare thus in Luke 4

And he said to Him, To You I will give all this power and authority and their glory (all their magnificence, excellence, preeminence, dignity, and grace), for it has been turned over to me, and I give it to whomever I will. - Luke 4:6 AMP

Satan for once spoke the truth. He showed Christ the earth and said all of this power and authority has been turned over or transferred to me. Yes, Adam through sin had transferred authority to him. Yet wait for it for God was about to wrestle that authority from him and turn it back to man. The first Adam turned his authority over to Satan but the second Adam – Christ beat him, took the authority and gave it back to man. Listen to what Christ said

Jesus approached and, breaking the silence, said to them, all authority (all power of rule) in heaven and on earth has been given to Me. - Matthew 28:18 AMP

The authority that Satan promised to give if Christ will bow and worship him had been taken from him. Satan is still lying to the world and they are still believing his lies. He promises the people of the world that he will give them influence, power, affluence and authority if they will worship him. Deception. He can't give what he don't have. The world don't know that authority is not his (Satan) to give so they continue to be deceived. Satan has been stripped of all spiritual authority that he stole from Adam. What he gives is counterfeit of the real thing and it is doomed to fail always. He has been defeated and stripped of all authority. Again Jesus told his disciples

Jesus came to them and said: I have been given all authority in heaven and on earth! - Matthew 28:18 CEV

All means all. Satan don't have any authority to give you or anyone. He lies. He can give you counterfeit authority but it will not endure. He has been stripped of all authority

And having disarmed the powers and authorities, he made a public spectacle of them, triumphing over them by the cross. - Colossians 2:15 NIV

He disarmed devils. He took away their authority. Not only did He take away authority from them He also handed that authority back to man. In addition he made redeemed man to have authority or dominion over darkness. You my dear child of God have been given authority- exousia (the power to rule, have influence, and exercise control) over Satan and all power of darkness. The authority you have received empowers you to rule over the forces of darkness. Christ beat Satan at the cross, redeemed us out of his hands and placed us where we rightly belong over him. In Christ we have authority to lord it over Satan and darkness.

Behold, I give unto you power to tread on serpents and scorpions, and over all the power of the enemy: and nothing shall by any means hurt you. - Luke 10:18-19

I say it again because the word of God says so. Satan has been beat. He is defeated. Christ thumped him and gave us authority- exousia over him and all his kingdom and his works. We are to rule- trample over snakes and scorpions- witches, demons and all forces of darkness.

After Christ had delegated authority or exousia to them in Luke 9 they came back rejoicing saying the demons are subject to them- the disciples.

The seventy-two returned with joy and said, "Lord, even the demons submit to us in your name."- Luke 10:17NIV

Just like you are subject to the orders of the traffic warden when you get to a traffic junction so too devils are subject to your orders because heaven has given you authority over them. Use the authority you have been given to subdue and bring into submission every work of darkness and evil opposing you. Let darkness, disease, poverty and failure submit to you in Jesus. Unleash your God given authority upon the enemy that has been fighting your destiny.

God put a rod- symbol of authority in the hands of Moses and all of Egypt could not stop him. With the rod of spiritual authority God gave him he was able to unleash his ministry accompanied with signs and wonders upon the Egyptians and release the captive nation of Israel. The magicians of Egypt could not stand Moses and Aaron because their own authority was inferior to the one the men of

God carried. Darkness will always bow to light. Light will always beat darkness. The power of darkness will always submit to the power of God.

God had given Gideon spiritual authority but Gideon did not know. And because he did not know he lived all his life in fear. He was troubled, harassed and victimized by what he should have been putting down using the higher authority that had been given him by God. The day his eyes opened he turned from the pursued to the pursuer.

And his comrade replied, this is nothing else but the sword of Gideon son of Joash, a man of Israel. Into his hand God has given Midian and all the host. - Judges 7:14 AMP

The sword of Gideon- authority. When David went to confront Goliath he picked up his staff- authority. Hear what the word of God says in John 1:12 in the amplified translation

But to as many as did receive and welcome Him, He gave the authority (power, privilege, right) to become the children of God, that is, to those who believe in (adhere to, trust in, and rely on) His name—John 1:12 AMP.

That settles it. The word of God is the standard. The word of God settles every controversy. He gave them authority to become. Become what. Authority to become what God wants you to become. Authority to unleash the greatness that He deposited on their inside. Authority to manifest their sonship status. You don't have any reason to stay down when you have been given authority to be successful, great and so much more. Moses with this authority from God moved from being the "son of pharaoh" to a lowly shepherd of his father in law's sheep and finally to the great leader and deliverer of Israel. God used him to wrought many miracles and brought the children of Israel out of Egypt. Moses achieved greatness and you too can achieve greatness. You have the same God Moses had. Same power and same authority too.

And Moses was learned in all the wisdom of the Egyptians, and was mighty in words and deeds. - Acts 7:22 NKJV

Moses was mighty in word and deed. He had the same God you have. He achieved greatness and you too can be mighty in word and deed. You can achieve greatness. Don't stop till you become great. You have received Doonamis (power) and exousia (spiritual authority) to become successful and great. A giant was lying asleep inside Gideon with all the Doonamis (power) and exousia (authority) he possessed. The giant had to awaken and rise up. The warrior in him had to be unleashed and boy did he unleash the giant or warrior inside him. The giant in him awakened and he was unleashed upon the Midianites.

The same power and authority Gideon had you have also received from God. Don't die before you become successful and great. Don't stop at your current level. Go higher until you reach the topmost top that God has planned for you. Where you are now should be the least you will be. Keep moving ahead. Keep moving upward. Keep moving forward. Isaac prospered, continued to prosper until he became very prosperous.

The man began to prosper, and continued prospering until he became very prosperous; - Genesis 26:13 NKJV

It's your turn to prosper for you are next in line to achieve success and greatness. The giant in you can't stay asleep anymore. God is unleashing the giant in you. The warrior in you is set to war and conquer. This is your season. You were born for such a time as this. Your world has been waiting for the giant inside you to arise and conquer. Power and authority has been given to you by God. The unlimited power of God is with you and for you. So you can't be stopped. You are like the wind and can't be stopped or hindered.

The wind blows where it wishes, and you hear the sound of it, but cannot tell where it comes from and where it goes. So is everyone who is born of the Spirit." - John 3:8 NKJV

God is seeking willing and available vessels. Will you yield yourself to Him? Vessels for His power and authority so that they can be battle axes in His able hands to defeat and drive further back the kingdom of darkness.

It's time to succeed and be great. It's time to unleash the winner that has been lying dormant inside you. For the sake of your world and to the glory of God that warrior or winner in you needs to come forth. The winner in you needs to arise and shine. The giant inside you needs to manifest and influence your world. There is what you have that your world needs. Give it to them. Let the world meet the warrior inside you. He can't remain hidden or trapped any longer. It's time to unleash the giant in you.

6

ON PURPOSE WITH A PURPOSE

The purpose of life is to live a life of purpose. – David Roads

"*God makes each one of us for the time into which we are born. He creates us for a purpose. Our job is to know Him well, discover what He created us to do, and then do it for all we're worth for the rest of our lives. Ask God to show you your purpose. He will answer.*" – **Robin Lee Hatcher**

6.1 You are fearfully and wonderfully made

Gideon did not rate himself very much. He considered himself small and insignificant. He considered himself as weak and good for nothing. He even considered his family weak, small, nothing and incapable of anything good. He felt small and so he lived small. Thinking too highly of oneself is as bad as thinking too lowly of yourself. That was Gideon the warrior. Think it and you will become it. It is hard to succeed or win in life when you think poorly about yourself. No wonder the word of God says in Proverbs 23:7 in the King James Version:

For as he thinketh in his heart, so is he: Eat and drink, saith he to thee; but his heart is not with thee.

You become what you think. You can't rise higher than you think. As you think you will become. You can't think low and rise high. Your thinking affects your level in life. God had to rearrange Gideon's thinking and boost his confidence. To win in life you must be confident in God and confident in yourself. One confident person in the bible is David. Hear him in Psalm 139:14

I will praise thee; for I am fearfully and wonderfully made: marvelous are thy works; and that my soul knoweth right well.

Man is God's most excellent creation. God spared no expense so to say when He created man. Man was the last but the best of God's creation. And of all God's creation it was only man that was created in His image and likeness. Even angels were not created in God's image. Sin may have corrupted the nature of man but still after Christ redeemed man from sin and restored him back to union with God, that original glory of man is given back to man. Sin caused man to fall short of the glory of God but praise God that through Christ man is restored to that original glory. Little wonder the apostle describes the new creation in such glorious fashion in 2 Corinthians 5:17

Therefore if any man be in Christ, he is a new creature: old things are passed away; behold, all things are become new.

If any man is in Christ he is a new creature. Old things of sin, failure, disease, weakness are passed away. In Christ you are not the old, weak, good for nothing, no future ambition person others think you are. Or perhaps even you have like Gideon come to believe that about yourself. The things of old have passed away. You can be confident in God and in your God given ability. You are a new creature. Special in the sight of God and beloved of God. Before verse 17 hear what 2 Corinthians 5:16 GW translation has to say

So from now on we don't think of anyone from a human point of view. If we did think of Christ from a human point of view we don't anymore-

Don't see yourself as men see you rather see yourself as God sees you. Whenever Gideon looks at himself he sees weakness, smallness, doubt, limitation but whenever God looks at him all God sees is strength, might, power. God sees you as a mighty man of valour or warrior. A winner. You are a winner. Men see on the outside but God sees inside. Men see who you are but God sees who you can be. God should know because He created you. Men don't know you even though they think they do. It should not surprise you because no man is your creator.

Learn to see yourself as God sees you. See yourself as the **word of God** sees you not as the **world** or opinions of men see you. Don't look at yourself from a human point of view rather look at yourself from a divine point of view. Men can devalue you but God values you. You are not who men say you are rather you are who God says you are and that you agree that you are. Again the Apostle Paul tells us that

For we are his workmanship, created in Christ Jesus unto good works, which God hath before ordained that we should walk in them. - Ephesians 2:10

We are God's hand work created in Christ Jesus unto good works which He ordained that we should walk in them. We have been recreated in Christ Jesus to walk successful, walk victoriously and walk in greatness. Don't settle for less. Settle for the best of God for you. The man Israel prospered, continued to prosper until he became very prosperous- Genesis 26:13 NJKV. God wants you to walk healthy, walk successful, walk prosperously and walk in greatness. You are fearfully and wonderfully made to walk fearfully and wonderfully too. Anything less than this is to fall short of God's ordination or plan for your life.

We are created anew for good works. We are created new creations. In Christ you are not the old you that was bound by sin, weak and a victim. He is the Potter and we are the clay. The Potter does not make nonsense or junk. You are God's property. A royal priesthood. A holy nation. A chosen generation. That makes you special.

But ye are a chosen generation, a royal priesthood, an holy nation, a peculiar people; that ye should shew forth the praises of him who hath called you out of darkness into his marvelous light- 1Peter 2:9

The world may not think you are special but God thinks you are special. The world may think lowly of you but God thinks highly of you. Mother, father and friends may abandon you but God said He will never leave you nor forsake you.

For thus saith the LORD of hosts; after the glory hath he sent me unto the nations which spoiled you: for he that toucheth you toucheth the apple of his eye. - Zechariah 2:8

You are the apple of God's eye. You belong to Him and are valuable to Him. You are so valuable that God was willing to sacrifice His only Son to redeem you back to Himself. Believe in God and believe in yourself. Believe in God's ability through you. Until you are confident in God and in who you are in

God you cannot unleash your best. You cannot unleash the "warrior" in you while thinking like one who is a victim. You are God's masterpiece. And you are created to perform good works. Believe that you are God's masterpiece created to walk in good works that he has ordained that you walk in. God had to reprogram Gideon's thinking before he was able to unleash the warrior in him. It is your turn to unleash the hidden winner- (singer, teacher, inventor, prophet, dancer, sportsman, president or that which God ordained you to walk in). And you will.

6.2 Everything and everyone has a purpose

You are not an accident or a mistake. God does not make mistakes and that is what makes Him so dependable. It is also among the numerous things that distinguish God from man. Man is not and can never be God and sure enough God is not a man. Why were you born at such a time as this? Why are you alive in this generation and not in some former generation or a latter generation? God placed you in the generation you have found yourself for a divine purpose. What are you alive for? Why are you alive for such a time as this? You are alive for a reason and for such a season as this. That was the critical statement Mordecai made to his cousin Esther.

If you keep quiet at a time like this, help will come from heaven to the Jews, and they will be saved, but you will die and your father's family will come to an end. Yet who knows- maybe it was for a time like this that you were made queen-Esther 4:14 GNT

Esther had just risen to the throne by the grace of God and she imagined that her being queen was so that she can wear fancy clothing, attend gala nights, luncheons and parties. She thought that it was a time to have servants be at your beck and call and for her to just enjoy being queen. Her much older and wiser cousin Mordecai reminded her that this was not so. God's purpose for your life is the reason you have life. You are alive to fulfil God's plan or purpose for your life. It's not the job or the money or titles you have. It's not the toys-cars, houses, clothes and jewelry. It is not even your physical or emotional comfort. All of these are good but they are secondary. Your God given purpose is what is primary. Jesus Christ reminded the disciples that His meat is to do the Father's will (purpose, plan, intention, design)

Jesus saith unto them, my meat is to do the will of him that sent me, and to finish his work. - John4:34.

You are not in this earth forever. You are sent to do a work or an assignment. Your chief or major task is to start and finish that work that your creator sent you to do in the earth.

Jesus said: My food is to do what God wants! He is the one who sent me, and I must finish the work that he gave me to do. - John4:34 CEV.

You are sent by God and you have a work to finish here on earth. God spoke to the prophet Jeremiah 1:5

Before I formed thee in the belly I knew thee; and before thou camest forth out of the womb I sanctified thee, and I ordained thee a prophet unto the nations.

Sanctified- set apart, chosen or selected and ordained for success and greatness. God had a divine plan or purpose for Jeremiah. That ordination was that he would be a prophet of God. Find your ordination from God and give it your all. Find your God given life call and give it your all. God ordained Jeremiah as a prophet to the nations. Nations and people would have suffered if Jeremiah did not fulfill his ordination or calling. Jeremiah would have been called a failure if he did not live and complete his ordination from God.

Concerning John the Baptist God spoke to His parents and said

For he shall be great in the sight of the Lord, and shall drink neither wine nor strong drink; and he shall be filled with the Holy Ghost, even from his mother's womb. And many of the children of Israel shall he turn to the Lord their God. And he shall go before him in the spirit and power of Elias, to turn the hearts of the fathers to the children, and the disobedient to the wisdom of the just; to make ready a people prepared for the Lord. – Luke 1:15-17

In three verses the angel from God declared John's divine purpose or ordination or assignment in the earth. Success and greatness in the sight of God depended on him (John) completing this particular assignment that God had commanded even before he was conceived in his mother's womb. And the angel goes ahead to say that he (John) shall be great in the sight of the Lord-verse 15. His success and greatness depended on whether he completed his God given task or ordination or calling.

You have not succeeded if you do not accomplish your God given assignment or calling in life. So you see, success in God's eyes is not measured by the kind of car you drive or the house you live in. Success and greatness in the eyes of God depends on you fulfilling divine purpose or assignment or ordination. Success in the eyes of the world is not success in the eyes of God. As you attempt to unleash the warrior-winner in you be sure you are attempting to do and excel at what God designed you to do. True excellence, success and greatness is only possible with God and doing that which He created you to do.

Before you were born God designed what you would do here on earth. It is called your purpose. Finding and doing what you were created by God to do is key to your success, happiness and ultimately fulfilment in life. There are too many sad and unfulfilled rich men and women around. That's is because money don't bring fulfilment. Living for God and doing what you were designed to do by God is what brings fulfilment. Frustration comes when you thought acquiring the "toys" will bring you happiness and satisfaction only to discover like Solomon that all is vanity.

Vanity of vanities, saith the preacher; all is vanity. - Ecclesiastes 12:8

God is the creator of the universe. Everything in the universe was created by God. Similarly God created everything with a purpose in mind. The sun was created with a purpose in mind. So too the moon and the stars. Everything in creation was created with a purpose by the creator. Satisfaction and happiness will only come when you align yourself with the purpose of the creator for you. Vexation or frustration comes when you are pursuing what is not his purpose for your life. You may reach the goal but instead of joy it lives a bitter taste in your mouth. You thought you would be happy only to get it and still find that you are not happy.

God had a purpose for Gideon. God's purpose for him was that he would be a warrior-winner. God's purpose was that he would be used of God to deliver God's people from the oppression of the Midianites.

And the LORD looked upon him, and said, go in this thy might, and thou shalt save Israel from the hand of the Midianites: have not I sent thee? - Judges 6:14.

All other things are but secondary. This is the major thing. Every other thing is minor. Succeed in the major and he will be termed to have succeeded. Fail at this one and succeed at all the other things and he would be termed a failure. You are born for a purpose that existed even before you were formed in your mother's womb. Some are ordained prophets like Jeremiah, ordained musicians like David, or ordained to prepare the way for the Lord like John, and some others are ordained deliverers like Moses. You have an ordination from God to fulfill.

There is a warrior-winner inside you like we have been saying all along. Your chief task in life is to unleash that warrior-winner inside of you. Your world is waiting for you to unleash the warrior-winner inside you and to be all that God planned for you to be and to do. Everything and everyone that God created was created on purpose and for His purpose. Live for Him and for His purpose for your life. Gideon the warrior was living life as a "thresher" because he did not know he was born to be a warrior. There was a warrior-winner hidden inside him that needed to be turned loose. To win in life he had to live his calling to be a warrior. As a thresher of wheat he will not have lived a winning life. You can only win at God's purpose for your life. Don't die threshing wheat when you should be warring and thrashing the enemy. Don't remain a victim when you can live life a victor. Don't settle for life as the conquered when you have been made more than a conqueror.

You are better than this and your present level is the least level you will ever be. Let the warrior-winner trapped in you be loose in Jesus name. You can be everything that God wants you to become and you can do everything He wants you to do. What He wants you to become is His purpose for your life. What He wants you to do is His purpose for your life. You are possibly wondering how you can discover His purpose for your life. Again this is not the place to exhaust this issue of divine purpose but I have one short answer for you. Live for God. Walk with Him. Delight yourself in Him. He will show (reveal it) you for the word of God has this to say.

But as it is written, Eye hath not seen, nor ear heard, neither have entered into the heart of man, the things which God hath prepared for them that love him. But

God hath revealed them unto us by his Spirit: for the Spirit searcheth all things, yea, the deep things of God. - 1Corinthians 2:9-10.

He wants to reveal His purpose for your life so you can live out His purpose for your life. Yes it comes by revelation. Your parents can't show you. Gideon looked at his life through the eyes of his parents and that is why he believed that he was the smallest in a family of small people. Smallest among the small. God revealed his true purpose to him. Your teachers at school can teach you but they can't reveal God's purpose for your life. The beautiful thing about His purpose for your life is that He wants to reveal it to you and He even said if you ask He will show you

Call unto me, and I will answer thee, and shew thee great and mighty things, which thou knowest not. - Jeremiah 33:3

Connect with this God and stay connected. Walk and keep walking with Him. He will reveal His purpose for your life. When you discover that purpose give it your best shot. Give it your all and don't settle for anything less than success and greatness. Unleash your all. Unleash the warrior-winner - architect, author, dancer, soccer player, preacher, healer, prophet, policeman, inventor etc. You want to know my own definition of success? Being the person that God wants you to be and doing what God wants you to do. It is being the very best that God wants you to be and doing your best at what God wants you to do.

6.3 What were you born to do?

And Methuselah lived after he begat Lamech seven hundred eighty and two years, and begat sons and daughters. And all the days of Methuselah were nine hundred sixty and nine years: and he died. - Genesis 5:26-27

What a waste. Methuselah lived nine hundred and sixty nine years on earth and the only achievement written to his name was that he fathered sons and daughters. Lived so many years on earth but did so little with his many years. His years were many yet only one accomplishment is written against his name- He begat. Indeed a waste of time, a waste of space and a waste of God's air. Lived so long yet achieved nothing.

Contrast Jesus Christ. He lived only 33 years yet did more in three years than Methuselah did in 969 years. I want to assume he (Methuselah) missed out on fulfilling his purpose. God had a purpose for him like he has a purpose for everyone. Jesus Christ was and still is a model to follow. Only 33 years in the earth but He accomplished God's purpose for His life and even more. Forever the world will not forget His exploits.

And there are also many other things which Jesus did, the which, if they should be written every one, I suppose that even the world itself could not contain the books that should be written. Amen. – John 21:25

See what He did in 33 years of living on earth. He might not have lived a long life the way we humans have come to understand living long but His exploits and achievements cannot all be written down in a book. He accomplished what He was born to do and even more. That is success. A car that flies has failed because the original intention of the manufacturer for it is not to fly. You succeed when you fulfil the intention or purpose that the creator has for you. You succeed when you do what you were born to do. Matthew 2:2 GNT has this to say concerning Jesus

And asked, "Where is the baby born to be the king of the Jews? We saw his star when it came up in the east, and we have come to worship him." -Matthew 2:2 GNT.

The wise men came to seek the baby who was born to be king of the Jews. His destiny or purpose in life was not settled **after** He was born. His destiny was settled **before** He was born. His destiny or what he was born to do was not settled after He grew up and became an adult. His destiny was decided before He was born. What He would be and do in the earth was settled by God before He was even conceived in His mother's womb. He was born to be the king of the Jews. His future was settled or determined by God before he was born even conceived. He was born to be king, ruler, Messiah, Savior. And now after He had conquered Satan he sits on the throne as King

Looking unto Jesus the author and finisher of our faith; who for the joy that was set before him endured the cross, despising the shame, and is set down at the right hand of the throne of God. - Hebrews 12:2

It's the same thing with you. There is something you were born to do. You have not succeeded if you do everything and don't do what you were born to do. What you were born to do is what you should be doing. At least you must do what you were born to do before you depart the earth. Your destiny or what you were born to do was settled by God before you were conceived. True success is to do what God has assigned you to do in the earth before you arrived the earth. It's called purpose. Life lived without fulfilling your God given purpose is a wasted life. Life that fulfills God's purpose is a celebrated life. Plan to live a **celebrated** life not a **wasted** life.

We all have something we were born to do. He has a purpose for your life and until you fulfill that purpose you have not succeeded. The apostle Paul who was a reformed murderer and now apostle and unrepentant preacher of the same gospel he was persecuting said it so well in Galatians 1

But when it pleased God, who separated me from my mother's womb, and called me by his grace, to reveal his Son in me, that I might preach him among the heathen; immediately I conferred not with flesh and blood- Galatians 1:15-16

His (Paul) assignment in the earth was settled before he was conceived in his mother's womb. Your life will not be termed or described as a wasted one because you will do what you were born to do. As long as you get connected and stay connected with the One who created you and assigned an assignment to you, you will not have lived a wasted life. Success is living the purpose that God gave you before you were born. Find what you were born to do, work at it with all you have, succeed at it and you would not have wasted your life. What you are born to do is something you must do before you leave this earth.

6.4 Succeed on purpose

And the LORD looked upon him, and said, Go in this thy might, and thou shalt save Israel from the hand of the Midianites: have not I sent thee? - Judges 6:14

God said to Gideon- go in this thy might and you shall save Israel from the hand of the Midianites. What an awesome God we serve. Gideon has not even agreed to take up the assignment yet God is already speaking that He will succeed in the assignment. He is not yet fully convinced that he is able to do the assignment yet God is talking of his success already. What was God saying? I have a purpose for you and as long as you walk in my purpose for you then you shall succeed. If you will walk in my (God) purpose for your life you will succeed. Success is true success when you succeed in God's purpose for your life. What the **world** calls success is not always what the **Word** calls success.

For my thoughts are not your thoughts, neither are your ways my ways, saith the LORD. - Isaiah 55:8

The world even measures success by how much fame or popularity you have. One wise person said Hitler had millions of followers but Jesus had 12 apostles during His time on earth. Does that make Hitler a success and Jesus a failure? No it does not. The world measures success with how much money, cars, houses and other material toys you are able to accumulate. Whether you steal it, borrow it, kill to have it or earn it legally or cleanly it does not matter in the eyes of the world. Just get it anyhow you can as long as you get it.

Jesus throws that kind of thinking to the trash can in many ways. In the parable of the rich fool, he (the rich man) thought he was successful because his ground brought forth abundantly.

And he said unto them, Take heed, and beware of covetousness: for a man's life consisteth not in the abundance of the things which he possesseth. - Luke 12:15

Money will never bring you lasting happiness and fulfilment. Living and acquiring toys- cars, gold, jewelry, houses, fashion or expensive clothing will never bring you happiness and fulfilment. Knowing and living out God's purpose for your life is what will bring you happiness and satisfaction. When you have done the will of God you will find happiness, fulfilment and be able to say like Apostle Paul

I have fought a good fight, I have finished my course, I have kept the faith- 2 Timothy4:7

These are the words of a man who as they say came, saw and conquered. Fulfilment comes from fulfilling God's purpose for your life. Paul had finished the course God gave him. He had run the race that God had given him to run. The good fight God gave him he had fought and he had won. Yes, He had succeeded on purpose. Gideon's God given purpose was to thrash the

Midianites oppressing God's people and set him free. He accomplished just that. He too succeeded on purpose.

God created everything on purpose and with a purpose. God is not confused. God is focused and He knows what He is doing. On purpose He created everything and everything was created with a purpose. If you must be considered successful you must succeed on purpose. Everything God created was on purpose and for a purpose. There is nothing God created that did not have a purpose. He made everything on purpose for a purpose. I can't think of anything He created that does not have a purpose, because there is none. Can you? Tie success to God's purpose for your life.

You succeed not by doing everything but by doing everything that God has planned for you to do. John succeeded because it was written concerning him that- the voice of one crying in the wilderness and making or preparing the way for the coming Messiah.

He said, I am the voice of one crying in the wilderness, Make straight the way of the Lord, as said the prophet Esaias. - John 1:23

Be a voice not an echo. Find your path in life and walk in it. Don't be an imitation or copy. Make your own brand and be yourself. Lazy people are those who want to be other people and not themselves. They are so busy trying to be others and end up not being anyone or anything useful. They did not become who they tried copying or imitating and they did not become who or what God planned for them to become. Failure. You did not achieve being the original you God planned that you become and you did not achieve being the copy of others you wanted to become. Christ who is our role model and mentor had this to say concerning himself

When Jesus therefore had received the vinegar, he said, it is finished: and he bowed his head, and gave up the ghost. - John 19:30

He had finished his assignment, his mission on earth and the Father's purpose for His life. Only then did He give up the Ghost. He was not permitted to die until He had finished the race that His Father had given Him to run. Until He had completed the course that was assigned to Him He was not permitted to die and He did not. Let me prophesy over you that you are not permitted to die until you have finished running your race. You can't be killed. There is a course to finish and you will finish it. There is a finish line waiting for you and you will reach it in Jesus name. Amen. Get ready to finish your course or race for you will. Get ready to succeed on purpose because you will succeed on purpose.

RESPONSIBILITY

7

TAKE RESPONSIBILITY

The price of greatness is responsibility- Winston Churchill

God will not do it all. There is always a God part and there is always a human part to play. God is always faithful to play His part. All the time it is always man that did not play his part. God is too God not to be faithful. God is not less than faithful. He is more than faithful to play His part. Are you faithful to play your own part?

You and God are partners for your move towards success and greatness. You can be all that God wants you to be and do all He wants you to do. God will not fail you but are you ready to play your own part. Your own part is your responsibility. God's part is His responsibility. Play your own part. Take responsibility for your own responsibility. Nothing just happens rather things happen because something or someone made things to happen. If you will take responsibility, your life will not remain the same. You will achieve success and reach greatness. You will unleash the warrior-winner hidden inside you. One man asked a very critical question when he asked- what must I do to be saved?

And brought them out, and said, Sirs, what must I do to be saved? – Acts 16:30

This chapter will deal with the question of what must I do to unleash the warrior-winner in me. What must I do to become all that God wants me to become and to do all that God wants me to do? We will answer the question- What must I do to unleash the winner in me?

7.1 You must be saved

That you need to be saved needs to be stressed over and over and over again. Salvation in Christ is the foundation or root of true success and greatness. Salvation is what positions you to live a life of true success and greatness. To be the person that God created you to be and to do everything He has called you to do you must be reconciled to your creator. In fact Jesus Christ said you **must** be born again. To be everything the creator created you to be you must walk with the creator. To do the works of God you must walk with God. To do the work He sent you to do in the earth you must walk with God. You cannot unleash the fullness of who you are in God if you do not walk with God.

Rebels don't prosper because the word of God says the rebellious dwell in a dry land.

God setteth the solitary in families: he bringeth out those which are bound with chains: but the rebellious dwell in a dry land. – Psalm 68:6

To succeed and be great in life you must be connected to the source of greatness-God. To be great you need another to make you great. God is great and He is able to make you great. Salvation is much more than you are saved and are going to heaven. It is not sitting in church and singing hymns. It is all that and more. You must be born again because that is what will grant you ability to become what God wants you to become and to do all He wants you to do. Jesus said to the early apostles

And he saith unto them, Follow me, and I will make you fishers of men. – Matthew 4:19

To become all He wants you to become and to do you must follow Him. You must walk with Him. You must submit to Him. Your purpose without following the one who determined that purpose for your life is impossible to attain. He called the disciples to him and gave them power and authority but first they had to obey His call.

Jesus called the twelve disciples together and gave them power and authority to drive out all demons and to cure diseases. - Luke 9:1 GNT.

The born again experience or spiritual rebirth is much more than I am saved and going to heaven. It is not religion. The born again experience is the foundation for total turnaround in the life of any man or woman that will accept Christ as their LORD and Savior. Salvation grants you unhindered access into the kingdom and the right to share in the inheritance of those that are in the kingdom of light.

Jesus answered and said unto him, Verily, verily, I say unto thee, except a man be born again, he cannot see the kingdom of God. – John 3:3

Forgiveness of sins through repentance and acceptance of the free gift of salvation grants you access to the kingdom of God and your inheritance in the kingdom. You really **MUST** be born again if you must unleash the best of all that God has deposited inside you. If you are not born again or know Christ as Savior you need to make the following prayer

Father in heaven I am a sinner. I repent of my sins. Forgive me, cleanse me from sin, make me your child and fill me with your Holy Spirit in Jesus Name. Amen. Thank you for forgiving me my sin and making me your child.

Next thing to do is to get a bible and start to read daily. Pray that God will lead you to a bible believing church close to you where you can submit to the pastor and grow in the faith. Your journey to true success and greatness just begun. Now you will see what God will do with and in your life.

7.2 Have the faith of God

And Jesus answering saith to them, have faith of God- Mark 11:22 YLT

Victors need faith to emerge victorious. Winners, warriors, overcomers need faith. You need the faith of God to unleash the best of God from inside you. Faith is a must if you must unleash the warrior-winner in you. Faith that trusts in the ability of God. We are not talking about normal or human faith. We are talking about the faith of God. Everyone has some level of faith but not everybody has the faith of God. Why do people go to a job from the beginning of the month and wait till the end of the month to get paid? They do so because they have faith that they will be paid at the end of the month.

You go to school and endure the discipline of reading and writing examinations because you have faith that you will be awarded a certificate at the end of the day. That is human faith and everyone has that. You enter a plane and believe it will take you to your destination. You even tell someone to wait and pick you at the airport before you arrive. What confidence or guarantee do you have that you will arrive? Faith. Natural faith. Everyone (Christian believer and unbeliever) has natural faith.

However there is another level of faith called the God kind of faith or the faith of God but not everyone has that. The faith of God or the God kind of faith is faith that God imparts to those who are in His kingdom. Kingdom folk are expected to have Kingdom faith. That is why 1John5:4 says whatsoever is born of God overcomes the world through faith. If you are born again you have been born into the kingdom and God blesses you with the gift of supernatural faith. Only kingdom sons and daughters of God are able to demonstrate supernatural faith. Entrance into the kingdom of God grants you automatic access to the faith of God in a measure. This faith of God is supernatural faith. Not everybody has supernatural faith. It is a gift of God given to only those who are citizens of His kingdom

This supernatural faith that is the faith of God knows no limits. Natural faith has limitations but the supernatural or God kind of faith has no limitations. That is why Jesus Christ said:

Jesus replied, "Why do you say 'if you can'? Anything is possible for someone who has faith!" – Mark 9:23 CEV

Supernatural faith is indispensable if you must live the godly life or the kingdom life. What is a godly life? The godly life is the kind of life that God planned for you to live. 3 John 2 tells us what the godly life is

Beloved, I wish above all things that thou mayest prosper and be in health, even as thy soul prospereth.

The godly life is a life lived by the power of God through the faith of God. It is life lived with God and by the power of God. The godly life is not religion or a set of rules to live by. It is living an overcoming, all conquering life by the power of God. You need the power of God to live a godly life and that is why scriptures say that His divine power has given us all things that pertain to life and godliness.

According as his divine power hath given unto us all things that pertain unto life and godliness, through the knowledge of him that hath called us to glory and virtue- 2 Peter1:3

What is faith? Hebrews 11:1 says it is the substance of things hoped for. It is spiritual and unseen yet real and effective.

Now faith is the substance of things hoped for, the evidence of things not seen. - Hebrew 11:1

Believers are to walk by faith not by sight. Gideon had to learn to walk by faith. A faith that sees God and not the obstacles. It is a faith that is able to kill fear. Supernatural faith which drives out fear. Where there is faith there can be no fear and where there is no faith there will be fear. When the angel of God spoke the word of God to Gideon it inspired faith in Gideon. And that faith moved him to action and he conquered the Midianites. Faith is a must if you must live a conquering or overcoming life. You can't win without faith. You need faith to win the battles of this life.

For whatsoever is born of God overcometh the world: and this is the victory that overcometh the world, even our faith. - 1John 5:4

The child of God (one who is born of God) will encounter trials, opposition, challenges in the world but God has given him or her the gift of faith to help him/her overcome all such. There is nothing that the world will throw at you that you cannot overcome. There is no battle that God permits in your life that can defeat you. You are born to win but in other to win you need faith. With God and faith in God you can win. Gideon had to learn to live by faith.

Faith sees God not the problem. Faith people are winning people and winning people are faith people. Faith people believe in the ability of their God. They see God more than they see the obstacles in front of them. The rest of Israel saw Goliath as an obstacle that was too big for them but David saw God as bigger and that Goliath was an opportunity for the demonstration of what faith in the power of God can do. Obstacles or opposition are opportunities for the demonstration of the power of God. However it takes supernatural faith to activate the power of God to crush the obstacles. David believed in the ability of His God. Faith in God moves mountains. Faith in God moves obstacles.

Jesus replied, "Why do you say 'if you can'? Anything is possible for someone who has faith!" – Mark 9:23 CEV

These are the very words of Jesus. That anything is possible for someone who has faith!! Anything!! God- you mean anything is possible if I have faith! What is stopping you from succeeding is not the economy. It is not witches. It is your faith. Anything is possible. You can go as far as your faith will go. God will go as far as my faith will go. Listen to what God told Abraham

For all the land which thou seest, to thee will I give it, and to thy seed forever. – Genesis 13:15

God gifts you a measure of supernatural faith when you get saved and become a citizen of the kingdom. However you need to build on it (faith) and increase it even more. And that is where the word of God comes in for Romans 10:17 says

So then faith cometh by hearing, and hearing by the word of God.

Supernatural faith or the faith of God comes through hearing the word of God. Even though you have received a measure of faith you need to grow your faith and daily too. You grow your faith by hearing the word of God, meditating on it, confessing it and doing what it says. When you do it will inspire faith in you. And when faith comes nothing shall be impossible for you. Feed on the word of God daily and you will be growing your faith daily too. Man does not live by bread alone but by every word that proceeds from the mouth of God- Matthew 4:4. You need faith but to have faith you must feed on the word of God daily. God wants us to abound in faith. To abound in faith means to have faith in abundance.

Therefore, as ye abound in everything, in faith, and utterance, and knowledge, and in all diligence, and in your love to us, see that ye abound in this grace also. – 2Corinthians 8:7

Yet to abound in faith you must abound in the word of God for the word of God is the only source of supernatural faith. Do you want to live in the realm of supernatural faith? That realm where impossibility does not exist then you must abound in the word of God so that you can have the faith of God in abundance. Again Jesus speaking had this to say concerning faith

And Jesus said unto them, Because of your unbelief: for verily I say unto you, If ye have faith as a grain of mustard seed, ye shall say unto this mountain, Remove hence to yonder place; and it shall remove; and nothing shall be impossible unto you.- Matthew 17:20

Nothing is impossible for faith. If your faith says yes God won't say no. Faith in God destroys impossibility. The doctors said you cannot be healed. That is what their faith says. What is your own faith saying? Find the promise of God concerning healing and let it build faith on your inside. Anything is possible for God. Anything is possible for the word of God. And anything is possible for the believer who grabs the word of God and holds on to it. Doctors had told the woman with the issue of blood that she could not get healed but one day she touched Christ (the Word) and faith sprang up on her inside and she was healed. What the faith of men said was impossible became possible for her because of her supernatural faith in God.

And he said unto her, Daughter, be of good comfort: thy faith hath made thee whole; go in peace. - Luke 8:48.

Hebrews 11 is the account of men and women that did exploits with their faith and Gideon is mentioned among them. You are not great if you have not been mentioned in God's hall of faith. You have not succeeded if you have not been mentioned in God's hall of faith. Gideon's name entered the list of great people. And your name will enter that list too. That same list had great men like Joseph David, Solomon, Rahab, Moses, and Samson.

And what shall I more say? For the time would fail me to tell of Gedeon, and of Barak, and of Samson, and of Jephthae; of David also, and Samuel, and of the prophets. Who through faith subdued kingdoms, wrought righteousness, obtained promises, stopped the mouths of lions- Hebrews 11:32-33

These men and women did exploits with their faith in God. Supernatural faith or the faith of God is limitless. Ordinary men with extraordinary faith in God will always do exploits. See what Moses did in Egypt. See what a disciple called

Stephen did. Not an apostle or a bishop but see what he did all because he had supernatural faith

And Stephen, full of faith and power, did great wonders and miracles among the people. – Acts 6:8

By faith Stephen was empowered to do great wonders and miracles. You can do what Stephen did and even more. You can live the supernatural life of God. You can unleash the best of God for your life. Your world has not seen the best of God for your life but they will because God is set to unleash His best in your life. You have stayed average long enough. You faith will bear fruit. You have lived ordinary for too long and now it is time to live extraordinary. It's you season for breakthroughs. It's your season to unleash success and greatness from inside you. It's your turn to unleash the warrior-winner hidden inside you.

7.3 Open the Book

Jesus answered, "You're off base on two counts: You don't know your Bibles, and you don't know how God works. - Matthew 22:29 MSG

When we were kids we were told that if you want to drive away evil put a bible under your pillow when you go to sleep. Also at home the whole house would have only one bible- the family bible. Nobody read that family bible or if they did it was read once in a while. It was a mark of religion that every "Christian home" should decorate their book shelf with a big family bible even if nobody read it.

And off cause the devil is happy because he knows that a bible under your pillow is harmless to him. As long as the bible is not in your heart but under your pillow the enemy is comfortable. As long as the bible is on the bookshelf gathering dust the enemy is comfortable. What scares him is when you open the bible, read it, meditate it and plant the life giving words in your heart. He is scared because when you know what the bible says he can't stop you. When you don't know you remain bound.

Not knowing the bible keeps you bound, limited and restricted. Opening and knowing the bible (the truth) is what sets free, liberates and delivers your inheritance to you. The enemy is subtle and he will give you reasonable and unreasonable excuses for you not to open your bible. As long as you don't open and read and know he is safe. He knows that once you know that you know then he is not safe. Not knowing the bible is destructive and keeps you bound and limited. Move to open the bible regularly. Move to know so you can be set free and stay free. Satan can't stop you once you know your inheritance through opening the word of God. The truth will set you free and the word of God is the truth

And ye shall know the truth, and the truth shall make you free. – John 8:32

The word of God is alive and full of power- Hebrews 4:12. The word of God is able to transform your whole life. Once you have received the gift of salvation you need to feed on the word of God so that you might grow into your inheritance. The word of God reveals your inheritance in God.

And now, brethren, I commend you to God, and to the word of his grace, which is able to build you up, and to give you an inheritance among all them which are sanctified. - Acts 20:32

The word of God will build you up and give you an inheritance among the saints of God. God has prepared an inheritance for all His children. To receive your own inheritance you must know what is written and to know what is written you must open the book of the law. The word of God is the book of the law. Jesus Christ had to open the book and find what was written in the book concerning Him.

And there was delivered unto him the book of the prophet Esaias. And when he had opened the book, he found the place where it was written, -Luke 4:17

There is only one book in the universe that has ability to transform your life. This book has the ability to take you from where you are to where God wants you to be. There are books but this book is "The Book". This book is an all-time bestselling book. Down the ages men and kings have tried their very best to stop or destroy this book and they have failed. Instead the book has gone on from strength to strength. It's been translated into more languages than any other book. It has sold and continues to sell more copies than any book the world has known or will ever know. It's not surprising because this book has been authored or inspired by the Almighty God, the one true and only living God. The book is called the Holy Bible.

All scripture is given by inspiration of God, and is profitable for doctrine, for reproof, for correction, for instruction in righteousness – 2 Timothy 3:16

Jesus opened the book and found where it was written concerning Him. When He found it He declared that it is fulfilled. Until you find what is written in the book concerning you don't expect fulfilment. Finding requires effort. It requires you deliberately opening the bible, reading it, meditating in it, believing it and practicing it. As you do the Holy Spirit will reveal the mind and plan of God to you. As you do all this you will be transformed. The bible is not a story book it is a life transformer. You can't hope to make godly progress while ignoring the word of God.

Jesus opened the book and found where it was written concerning Him. If Jesus opened The Book you sure need to open The Book. Open the book and find what has been written concerning you. When you find His promise concerning you and believe it will be fulfilled. The Bible is not something you decorate your bookshelf with. It is that you might open it and discover what has been written concerning you.

So open the Book. The book is not meant to be kept under your pillow. Take the word of God and put it in your heart. The rule of godly success has not changed- This Book of the Law shall not depart from thy mouth. Open the book to read and your life will be transformed from one level to another. Don't only read the word. After you have read it meditate (ponder, think, digest) on what is written.

Oh how I love thy law! It is my meditation all the day- Psalm 119:97

Opening and reading the book gives you knowledge or information but meditating on what you have read gives you revelation. And when you have revelation of what is written the gates of hell will not be able to prevail against you. When you have revelation or understanding in the scripture not even hell can stop your transformation or change.

And Jesus answered and said unto him, Blessed art thou, Simon Barjona: for flesh and blood hath not revealed it unto thee, but my Father which is in heaven. And I say also unto thee, that thou art Peter, and upon this rock I will build my church; and the gates of hell shall not prevail against it. – Matthew 16:17-18

The word of God says my people perish for lack of knowledge- Hosea 4:6. They perish not because there is a devil out there but because they lack knowledge.

My people are ruined because they don't know what's right or true. Because you have turned your back on knowledge, I have turned my back on you priests. Because you refuse to recognize the revelation of God, I am no longer recognizing your children- Hosea 4:6 MSG

They rejected revelation and God in turn rejected them. It is revelation in the word of God that sparks transformation. When you meditate on the word of God the Holy Spirit will show you what the Father's will is and when you know what the father's will is nothing can stop you. Open the book, read and meditate. When you get revelation knowledge the word of God says you will be transformed.

And be not conformed to this world: but be ye transformed by the renewing of your mind, that ye may prove what is that good, and acceptable, and perfect, will of God. – Romans 12:2

When you find a promise in the word and you understand it there will be a performance of the promise. For we are told that not one of His promises in the word of God shall lack its mate. Every word of God in the bible has its mate in terms of the word being made flesh or performed.

Seek ye out of the book of the LORD, and read: no one of these shall fail, none shall want her mate: for my mouth it hath commanded, and his spirit it hath gathered them. – Isaiah 34:16

Some Christians are still living average, frustrated and defeated lives because they either do not open the book or open it too infrequently. We spend much time doing other activities, talking with friends, watching television and other secondary things while leaving the primary thing undone. Our lives are like that of Martha. We matter about many things and activities, even doing church work and ignoring that which is most needful. Mary made the right or wise choice. She sat at the Master's feet hearing the word of God.

And she had a sister called Mary, which also sat at Jesus' feet, and heard his word. But Martha was cumbered about much serving, and came to him, and said, Lord, dost thou not care that my sister hath left me to serve alone? Bid her therefore that she help me. And Jesus answered and said unto her, Martha, Martha, thou art careful and troubled about many things. But one thing is needful: and Mary hath chosen that good part, which shall not be taken away from her. - Luke 10:39-42

Mary heard the word. She sat at the feet hearing the word of the Master. When you spend time at the Master's (Christ's) feet hearing His word even the devil cannot be master(lord it) over you. Sickness cannot be a master over you when you have the word of Christ living in you. Sit at the Master's feet daily to hear His word. That is more important than running around to make a living.

After you have read and meditated on the word of God the next step is to do what the word of God says. Hearing and not doing what the word says will leave you not blessed. It is in hearing and doing that you are blessed. You do the word by confessing what you have heard. Agree that you are who the word says you are and that you can do whatever the word says you can do. Obey the word of God. Hearken to hear and to do and you will be blessed

Only be thou strong and very courageous, that thou mayest observe to do according to all the law, which Moses my servant commanded thee: turn not from it to the right hand or to the left, that thou mayest prosper whithersoever thou goest. - Joshua 1:7

It is only hearers and doers of the word of God that will be blessed. If the word says give and you shall receive then go ahead and give. If the word says forgive go ahead and forgive. The word says you are healed go ahead and believe you are healed even if the symptoms have not left you immediately. Fact can be changed but truth cannot be changed. What you are passing through is fact but the word of God is truth

Sanctify them through thy truth: thy word is truth. – John 17:17

The word of God is truth and cannot be changed. Circumstances of your life will change if you believe the truth (the word) even in the face of those circumstances looking like they will not change.

After you have read, meditated and believed the word of God the next step is to hold tight to the word you have received. Retain what you have heard because the enemy will come with intention to steal, kill and destroy what you have heard so that it will not bear fruit in your life.

Those by the way side are they that hear; then cometh the devil, and taketh away the word out of their hearts, lest they should believe and be saved. They on the rock are they, which, when they hear, receive the word with joy; and these have no root, which for a while believe, and in time of temptation fall away. And that which fell among thorns are they, which, when they have heard, go forth, and are choked with cares and riches and pleasures of this life, and bring no fruit to perfection. – Luke 8:12-14

Hold that which you have heard and believed for there is a thief waiting to steal what you have heard. The word of God is seed for your harvest of testimonies. Where there is no seed there can be no harvest. After the seed has been sown you need to hold unto the seed even in times of persecution and affliction. Hold the seed of the word of God in your heart until it bears fruit.

But that on the good ground are they, which in an honest and good heart, having heard the word, keep it, and bring forth fruit with patience. – Luke 8:15

The Apostles said it is not meet that they serve tables and ignore the ministry of prayer and the word. No wonder they shook their world. With the word of God you too can shake your world. They were unstoppable because they were students of the word.

Study to shew thyself approved unto God, a workman that needeth not to be ashamed, rightly dividing the word of truth. – 2 Timothy 2:15

Nothing can stop you if you abide in the word. Open the book. If Jesus needed to open the book, you sure need to open the book. Study to show yourself approved. Hear the good news of the gospel for this gospel is not mere words rather it is the power of God unto salvation for all that believe.

For I am not ashamed of the gospel of Christ: for it is the power of God unto salvation to everyone that believeth; to the Jew first, and also to the Greek. - Romans 1:16

Gideon got inspired when the angel spoke the word of God to him. The giant in him arose when he heard the word. The warrior-winner in him stood up when he heard the word and what was impossible for him became possible. Remember what the bible says in Acts 20:32.

And now, brethren, I commend you to God, and to the word of his grace, which is able to build you up, and to give you an inheritance among all them which are sanctified.

The word of God is able to build (strengthen, encourage, grow, develop) you and deliver your inheritance to you. It is thus a must that you open this book of the law continually. In the book is eternal life. In the book is supernatural ability to become all that God wants you to become and to do all that God wants you to do.

7.4 Prayer

Prayer is very important and it is very important to pray if you want to live a successful life. What is prayer? In simple terms prayer is talking to God. This book is not about prayer but prayer is definitely a need even a must if you must become all that God wants you to become and do all that God wants you to do. Prayer alone is not enough but prayer is sure very important. Look at what the Bible says in Jeremiah 33

Call to me, and I will answer you; I will tell you wonderful and marvelous things that you know nothing about. - Jeremiah 33:3 GNT

There are things about your life you don't know but God says call Him and He will answer you. He will show you wonderful and marvelous things you don't know. Your life can and should be wonderful and marvelous. God wants to do marvelous and wonderful things in your life as well as use you to do wonderful and marvelous things. He has a wonderful plan for your life. It is a plan to unleash success and greatness in your life.

I alone know the plans I have for you, plans to bring you prosperity and not disaster, plans to bring about the future you hope for. - Jeremiah 29:11 GNT

As you pray and commune with Him, God will unfold His plan for you and you can run with His plan for your life. It is only as you make His plan for your life your plan that you are guaranteed to succeed. Any other plan that is not His plan is guaranteed to fail.

There are many devices in a man's heart; nevertheless the counsel of the LORD, that shall stand. – Proverbs 19:21

It is in prayer and fellowship with Him that the Holy Spirit will reveal God's plan for your life.

But as it is written, Eye hath not seen, nor ear heard, neither have entered into the heart of man, the things which God hath prepared for them that love him. But God hath revealed them unto us by his Spirit: for the Spirit searcheth all things, yea, the deep things of God. - 1 Corinthians 2:9-10

Jesus Christ was a man of prayer. If Jesus who was the son of God prayed then who are you mortal man not to pray. Prayer is so important that John taught his disciples how to pray. In the same vein Christ's disciples asked that He teach them how to pray. And He did

One day Jesus was praying in a certain place. When he had finished, one of his disciples said to him, "Lord, teach us to pray, just as John taught his disciples." - Luke 11:1 GNT

Disciples of Christ ought to pray. Listen friends prayer is not a luxury it is a necessity. Even if you consider prayer a luxury it certainly is a luxury you cannot afford to do without. Psalm 65 says

O You who hear prayer, to you shall all flesh come. - Psalm 65:2 AMP

All is all. All flesh needs prayer and all flesh need to pray. If you are not prayerful you will be preyed upon. You probably have heard the saying that a prayer less Christian is a powerless Christian. You can't be a Christian and yet not pray. Children talk to their parents. If you are a child of God you ought to talk to your Heavenly Father. Prayer is extremely important. It is so important that Christ who was God in human flesh while on earth prayed. The bible gives account of Jesus praying on many occasions.

And in the morning, long before daylight, He got up and went out to a deserted place, and there He prayed. - Mark 1:35 AMP.

I love this. He got up long before dawn to pray. Obviously Christ was a man that was filled with the power of God. You would have thought that a man so powerful and capable of doing many miracles would not need prayer. Yet He prayed. You are not so powerful that you don't need prayer.

Even the powerful still need the help of God. Even the powerful still need direction and guidance. Even the powerful still need encouragement. Even the powerful still need to stay connected to the source of power for without Christ you can do nothing. Moses was mighty in word and deed because he had been given power and authority by God yet he was a man of prayer. David with all his exploits was a praying man. You can't be a succeeding man or woman if you are not a praying man or woman. Listen to what the word of God says in Psalm 65

By terrible things in righteousness wilt thou answer us, O God of our salvation; who art the confidence of all the ends of the earth, and of them that are afar off upon the sea. – Psalm 65:5

By terrible things in righteousness God will answer you. To get an answer you must first call. Until prayer has been made there can be no answered prayer. Are you ready for "terrible"- awesome; wonderful; beyond human comprehension things? Pray and don't stop praying. God did a "terrible" thing in the life of Paul and Silas after they had prayed and praised God in the prison. No prison is strong enough to hold you if you are given to prayer.

And at midnight Paul and Silas prayed, and sang praises unto God: and the prisoners heard them. And suddenly there was a great earthquake, so that the foundations of the prison were shaken: and immediately all the doors were opened, and every one's bands were loosed. – Acts 16:25-26

Again we see the power of God at work when the church prayed for Peter and the prison could not hold him back. The church prayed and the King of kings frustrated the intention of Herod for the life of Peter.

Peter therefore was kept in prison: but prayer was made without ceasing of the church unto God for him. And when Herod would have brought him forth, the same night Peter was sleeping between two soldiers, bound with two chains: and the keepers before the door kept the prison. And, behold, the angel of the Lord came upon him, and a light shined in the prison: and he smote Peter on the side, and raised him up, saying, Arise up quickly. And his chains fell off from his hands. - Acts 12:5-7

When Esther and her people prayed the evil intention of Haman was destroyed. Elisha was a man of similar passion (flesh and blood with human limitations) but he prayed. He prayed that it would not rain and it did not rain. Again he prayed that it should rain and the heavens gave rain.

Elias was a man subject to like passions as we are, and he prayed earnestly that it might not rain: and it rained not on the earth by the space of three years and six months. And he prayed again, and the heaven gave rain, and the earth brought forth her fruit. - James 5:17-18

Men ought to pray and not give up. Would be successful men pray and to succeed or become who God wants you to be you ought to pray. Pray! Pray! Pray! Pray till you succeed and become great. To win in life you must be a man or woman of prayer.

7.5 Obedience to God

Unrighteousness or disobedience blocks the power of God from being manifested or released in your life. Sin is a barrier. Sin stunted Adams rise and sin will stunt your rise in God. Sin is an enemy that you don't want to be found playing with. Sin is not your friend. If you want to be all God wants you to be you don't want to play with sin. Sin will always use and dump you. Sin will cut you off from God and His power. Without His power, grace and authority you can't unleash success and greatness. Sin is a "fire" you don't want to play with it. Sin will burn you. It will destroy your future in God. The biggest enemy of man is not the devil rather it is sin. Sin is not your friend. Sin is an enemy. Sin is an enemy of your success and greatness.

Sin has pulled down even the mightiest of men. Be brutal with sin. Cut sin off if you want to reach that place God ordained for you. To be a vessel unto God you must be holy and stay holy. Purge or force sin out of your life by the spirit of God which dwells in you. Sin corrupts the vessel. It blocks the vessel. You are God's vessel. A vessel of His power but it is your responsibility to keep the vessel clean, ready and meet for His use. Job hated sin and shunned evil and he was blessed by God.

There was a man in the land of Uz, whose name was Job; and that man was perfect and upright, and one that feared God, and eschewed evil. And there were born unto him seven sons and three daughters. His substance also was seven thousand sheep, and three thousand camels, and five hundred yoke of oxen, and five hundred she asses, and a very great household; so that this man was the greatest of all the men of the east. – Job 1:1-3

It was sin that cut Adam off from the presence and power of God. Sin will still do same today. Don't play with sin. Some started well but along the way sin cut short their progress. Start well, continue well and finish well and strong. There is nothing sin or the world has to offer you. It is sad that some started in the church and ended up in the world. Especially music people, entertainers and the like. It's common to read that he or she started out life by singing in the choir as a kid but ended up in the world.

They preferred to copy the way of the world. They preferred to fit or pattern their life according to the world instead of the word. Stay holy. Live holy. Holiness is a must. Don't be deceived by what the world says it can offer you. The world can offer you fame, riches, sex, position, drugs, alcohol and influence. Still what is the use of all of this if you lose your salvation in Christ?

What is the use of getting my name on Forbes list of the richest persons in the world and your name does not enter God's book of life. You can become the Time magazine man or woman of the year and still not get your name on the most important book you need your name to be in. You can be celebrated as the richest man in the world and yet not be rich towards God.

And whosoever was not found written in the book of life was cast into the lake of fire. – Revelations 20:15

Rich and powerful King Solomon said all is vanity. Man wants fame, recognition and to be celebrated but of what value is it for men to clap for me and God is not clapping for me. Listen pastor, preacher or man of God. You can't be righteous and unrighteous at the same time. You preach one thing but you do another. Preach righteousness and yet practice sin. Don't be carried away by the world. The world can't offer you anything lasting or enduring. You need the fear of God. When you have the fear of God you will abhor sin.

The fear of God spoke to Joseph when he had "opportunity" to sin with Potiphar's wife. His dream would have died the moment he gave in to that woman's seduction. Sin has killed or aborted more dreams than war and disease will ever do. Job was a righteous man because he eschewed (shunned) evil. Daniel and the other three Hebrew boys refused to defile themselves with the king's meat- sin. Many young people today are defiling themselves with sin, excess and wild living and in the process destroying their future in God.

Daniel and his friends refused to bow to sin by bowing to the king's idol. All of these people mentioned above, God honored their faith by making them great. They became heroes of faith who we can learn from. Some believers today do more talking than walking. They talk the Christian talk but they don't walk the Christian walk. Friends, brothers and sisters it is time to talk the talk as well as walk the talk. To become who we must be we must play by the rules of the **Word** and not by the rules of the world. Yes you read correctly- it is not a typo. Live by the principles of the word of God not by the principles of the world.

If we run with the world we will fall with the world but if we run with the word we will be what the word says we will be. It's your turn to be successful and great but you must walk in His word. Walk according to His word not according to the world. Shun, abhor, hate, and eschew sin. Have zero tolerance for sin. Holiness, righteousness, obedience to God is a must if we must be all that God wants us to be for no good thing will He withhold from those who walk uprightly before Him.

7.6 Dream, prepare, pursue

Where there is no vision, the people perish: but he that keepeth the law, happy is he- Proverbs 29:18

Gideon caught God's vision for his life. He discovered that God's vision was far greater than any vision or dream that he or his earthly father had for him. He thought God's vision for his life was to live and die a thresher of wheat. Your own vision for your life is small compared to God's vision for you. God's vision for your life is not to live and die a banker. It is far more than that. Left to Joseph's parents their vision for his life was to remain the "pet" of the house adored, pampered and spoiled. Left to Potiphar's wife her vision for Joseph's life was for him to remain the slave boy that refused to succumb to her temptations. Is your vision the same as God's vision for your life? Success that is hinged on any vision that is not God's vision for your life is failure. Don't be found trying to succeed in the wrong thing.

Gideon's vision was to thresh wheat. Whose life or how many lives will he have touched threshing wheat? God's vision for his life was to thrash Midianites and be a deliverer. He touched more lives when he embraced God's vision for his life. God wants you to be a blessing to families and nations yet you are there seeking to be blessed for yourself and perhaps your immediate family.

And I will bless them that bless thee, and curse him that curseth thee: and in thee shall all families of the earth be blessed. - Genesis 12:3

You need a vision or a dream for your life. Something that is bigger than you and that will require God to help you bring to pass. What better dream or vision than the one God has planned for you even before you were born? Catch God's dream for your life. People perish not for lack of money, connections or opportunities but for lack of vision. Your God given dreams are possible. Just make sure they are dreams that have been given you by God. Ambition is self and may not involve God and so chances of success with ambition are slim especially if it is of the destructive type. Adolf Hitler had ambition not purpose.

Ambition is different from purpose. Ambition many times blesses only you. For instance you want to buy a car. That is an ambition. Purpose on the hand could be that you want to establish a factory that makes cars and brings cars within the reach of many. Now that is obviously bigger than you and will definitely need God to help you accomplish. God has a dream that will touch you and touch lives- families, communities and nations. God will touch you and use you to touch lives. Remember that you are the light of the world.

Saul had been ruthlessly killing Christians until one day he had an encounter with Christ and he asked a question that changed the course of his life. He asked- what would you have me do.

And he trembling and astonished said, Lord, what wilt thou have me to do? And the Lord said unto him, Arise, and go into the city, and it shall be told thee what thou must do. – Acts 9:6

And the one who thought that God's vision for his life was to hunt down and kill Christians turned apostle. His (Saul) ambition was to be a "murderer" even if passively but God's purpose for him was that he be an apostle. Murderer was his ambition but God's dream or purpose for his life was to be a great apostle. He caught the dream and ran with it and the rest is history. He became a great apostle. You will accomplish God's purpose for your life. Catch his dream for your life and run with it

And the LORD answered me, and said, write the vision, and make it plain upon tables, that he may run that readeth it. - Habakkuk 2:2

God has a dream for your life. It's your responsibility to catch God's dream or vision for your life and run with it. Succeed with his vision for your life but to succeed with his vision for your life you will need to catch the vision and run wholeheartedly with it.

Prepare

Champions don't become champions IN the ring, they are merely recognized there. - John Maxwell

Champions or winners are not made inside the ring or on the field. They are made outside the ring/field but they manifest in the ring or field. Victors emerge victorious in the ring but they are victors before they enter the ring. Before they manifested in the ring there was a preparation period. There will always be a preparation period before the manifestation period. To write and pass an examination requires that the candidate first prepare to write the examination. Part of his/her preparation is hours of study, homework, researching and perhaps denial of sleep. All of that discipline is preparation if the candidate must manifest as one who passed the examination. To win you must prepare to win. God will prepare you and you will also be required to make preparation of your own.

God will prepare you

God will always prepare you for what He has prepared for you. Some of the preparation may not be pleasant but it is preparation you need to pass through. Esther had what it takes to be queen but she had to pass through a period of preparation.

Hegai liked Esther, and she won his favor. He lost no time in beginning her beauty treatment of massage and special diet. He gave her the best place in the harem and assigned seven young women specially chosen from the royal palace to serve her. - Esther 2:9 GNT

All the maidens selected to contest for the position of queen went through a preparatory period. Don't tell me it was fun. It was not fun but to emerge queen they had to submit to the discipline of preparation.

Good news translation of the bible describes it as beauty treatment. We all need this "beauty" treatment because all of us have some traits or "rough edges" that can hinder what God has called us to do. The king appointed Hegai to undertake or supervise the preparation of the maidens for possible selection as queen. In the same manner the LORD who is King of kings has appointed the Holy Ghost to prepare us for where and what He has prepared for us. That preparation often comes with pain, discipline, denying self and the flesh and much sacrifice. Your success and greatness will demand some sacrifice on your part.

God gave Joseph a dream of greatness. God showed him that He will make him great. He boasted to his brothers that his own parents and brothers will bow down to him. Like Esther he thought leadership was opportunity for others to serve him instead of him serving others. He imagined that leadership was a call to lord it over or dominate others. He was an arrogant and spoiled young man. God took him through a "school" of hard knocks to prepare him and trim off the rough edges in his character. He went through fire. Nothing purifies like the fire of affliction. He was first thrown into a pit, found himself in Potiphar's house and was later thrown into the prison. God brought him out from the prison and took him to the palace. The dream had come to pass but now he was a wiser, humble and better prepared man. The arrogant boy had matured into a humble man. He was no longer concerned with his brothers bowing down to him. Even when his brothers expected him to take revenge for what they had done to him, he did not take revenge. God had finished preparing him. His preparation was complete but it did not come easy.

God will prepare you for what He has prepared for you and sometimes He will have to take you through "fire".

Thou hast caused men to ride over our heads; we went through fire and through water: but thou broughtest us out into a wealthy place. - Psalms 66:12 KJV.

Your future includes a preparation time. Preparation time is not fun but in the end it is worth it. There will be a period of preparation between when God gives you the dream and when God fulfills the dream. It will be a time of waiting. It will even cause uncertainty to spring up in your mind if you let it. That is because it is a period when not much is happening. A wilderness or dry period when you look so far away from what and where God has planned for you. God however uses the wilderness to prepare His warriors, victors, conquerors, generals and triumphant sons and daughters. God prepared John the Baptist in the wilderness

And the child grew, and waxed strong in spirit, and was in the deserts till the day of his shewing unto Israel.-Luke 1:80

What was John doing in the desert? God was preparing him. He waxed strong in spirit. Only after then was he manifested publicly. Champions are made in secret but they manifest in the open. God used the desert to train, prepare and discipline him. Any disciple that has not passed through the discipline of preparation cannot manifest success and greatness.

God prepared David too. All the time David was "hidden" in the wilderness killing bears and lions, God was actually using to prepare him. His brothers didn't know so and even mocked him.

And Eliab his eldest brother heard when he spake unto the men; and Eliab's anger was kindled against David, and he said, Why camest thou down hither? And with whom hast thou left those few sheep in the wilderness? I know thy pride, and the naughtiness of thine heart; for thou art come down that thou mightest see the battle. - 1 Samuel 17:28

Few sheep and in the desert. If only Eliab knew that what he was calling few sheep and wilderness was actually being used by God to prepare David for future greatness. What you are passing through is preparation for the future God has planned for you. Endure the preparation.

God always prepares those He uses as His instruments or vessels. He prepared Moses for the great task of leading Israel out of Egypt. It was a preparation that lasted forty years. Wow! Similarly Jesus spent 30 years preparing for a 3 year ministry. Preparation must be very important in succeeding and ultimately achieving greatness.

God always prepares His vessels for what He has prepared for them. Preparation time or period may be long, dry and unpleasant but it is for your good. Jesus spent 30 years preparing for a 3year ministry. So much time spent preparing. No wonder he made so much impact while on earth. For thirty years He was an unknown carpenter's son and made no impact. God was still preparing Him for success, impact and greatness. Thirty for three! Spending thirty years preparing for a three year ministry. It shows you how important preparation for success and greatness is.

You look so far from the dream God showed you. Don't worry it's your preparation time. Thirty years preparing for a three year ministry. That was Jesus. For thirty years he was a carpenter's son unknown outside of his earthly father's village. A time came for his manifestation and the fulfilment of his ministry and assignment on earth. He could no longer be hidden. Exploits, signs and wonders began to happen in his ministry. The previously unknown Messiah was unleashing his ministry in the earth. The son of God was manifesting in full power and authority.

According to Mike Murdock - many would rather spend three years preparing for a 30year ministry. No wonder they do not make much of an impact with their ministry. Preparation time is learning time. It is equipping time if I can call it so. It is a period to learn to walk before you begin to run. We live in a world that is in a hurry. We want it and we want it yesterday. To enter and win a war you must be prepared adequately. The bible says which of you wanting to build a tower will not first of all sit down and count the cost.

For which of you, intending to build a tower, sitteth not down first, and counteth the cost, whether he have sufficient to finish it? – Luke 14:28

There is just no way a woman will conceive a baby and bring forth the baby on the same day or in an instant. God gave Joseph a dream of greatness at 17years old yet God spent the better part of 20 years preparing him for what He had prepared for him. David was in the wilderness slaying bears and lions. Little did he know that God was preparing him for bigger and greater exploits.

Do not despise your small place of exploits or achievements even if no one seems to be noticing them now. You just might be in the preparatory stage of your ministry or life. God does not use vessels that He has not prepared. For forty years Moses was in the wilderness caring for a few handful of sheep that belonged to his father in law. How could he have known that he would return to lead God's people through that same desert into the Promised Land? It was a training period that would come in handy later on as he led God's sheep through the wilderness. If you have not learned to care for Jethro's sheep surely God cannot trust you with Jesus' sheep. He that is faithful in little is going to be faithful in much.

You may be at a time in your life now that does not look glorious. You might be the associate pastor and so are not so much center stage as you would like. It don't matter, God is preparing you. Learn all you can learn now. For how you handle this phase determines whether you will enter the next phase. Young men today are desperate for instant success. Many today want to jump to the top rather than climb to the top. It's an error. That's the reason some individuals, companies, ministries or businesses are here today and gone tomorrow. They are like grass. Shallow roots and so easily pulled out. They are not like the palm tree. At the first scent of rain, the weeds are the first to spring up. Unfortunately they are gone as quickly as they appear. God is making a palm tree out of you. He will root you deep before He grows you tall. He will root you deep so that you can withstand storms and stay fruitful for a long time. So be patient and allow Him to have His way in your life. Remember what the bible says of the righteous.

And he shall be like a tree planted by the rivers of water, that bringeth forth his fruit in his season; his leaf also shall not wither; and whatsoever he doeth shall prosper. – Psalm1:3

God has prepared a place for you and He will take you there no matter what the state of your life is now. You are not there yet but He will take you there. You look so far away from your promised land but you will get there. God is not a liar. If He has spoken it, He will do it.

You may be at a place now that looks so far from the dream God showed you and it looks like the dream will not happen. God is still preparing you. You are in the wilderness or desert now and you are wondering how this thing can be. Fear not for you are passing through a preparatory phase in your life. God is preparing you for what He has prepared for you. Instead of despair and frustration you should celebrate and have the attitude of Job. Say like Job after He has taken me through the fire I will come forth as gold.

But he knoweth the way that I take: when he hath tried me, I shall come forth as gold. – Job 23:10

God also expects you to prepare for success and greatness

God will prepare you for what He has prepared for you but He also expects you to prepare for what He has prepared for you. There is what God will do and there is what you must do. Remember that you are a co-labourer or partner with God. God will prepare you for what He has prepared for you but He does not do it all. There is self-preparation that is required of you too.

So Jotham became mighty, because he prepared his ways before the LORD his God. -2Chronicles 27:6

Jotham prepared his ways before the LORD his God. He became mighty (great) because he prepared his ways before the LORD. He became successful and great because he prepared his ways before the LORD. He prepared for success and greatness by preparing his ways before God. There is a God preparation and there is a human preparation. Again God does not do it all. You prepare your ways before God. How do you prepare your ways before God? To succeed and be great you must prepare to succeed and be great. Success does not just happen. It is something you make happen. God will prepare you but there is preparation that is required on your part.

Jotham became mighty because he prepared his ways before the LORD his God. How did he prepare his way to success?

He prepared by seeking God and his ways. He walked with God. Seek first the kingdom of God and all other things shall be added to you. Seeking success and greatness should not be your primary goal in life. Your primary goal should be seeking the God who is able to make you successful and great. Like many a wise man would say- seek the Giver not the gifts. God desires that you know Him. Seek God above all other persons or things. Seek Him more than you seek money, fame, possessions or even success. Seek to know Him. That was Paul's prayer

That I may know him, and the power of his resurrection, and the fellowship of his sufferings, being made conformable unto his death- Philippians 3:10

Knowing Him is life. Knowing Him makes a huge difference. Knowing Him intimately or closely sets you up for victory, success and greatness. Pursue to know Him more than you pursue success and greatness. How did Jotham prepare his ways before God? He prepared by seeking the ways of God. God had a case against Israel in Isaiah 55:8-9

For my thoughts are not your thoughts, neither are your ways my ways, saith the LORD. For as the heavens are higher than the earth, so are my ways higher than your ways, and my thoughts than your thoughts.

Prepare for this God kind of success by seeking God and His ways always. The ways of God lead to the miracles of God. Moses knew the ways of God but the children of Israel knew the acts of God. Those that know the ways of God will be able to command the acts of God for it is the ways of God that lead to the acts of God. You can't be called successful if God is not in the center of your success. Success is in the eyes of the world may not be success in the eyes of God.

Jotham and his father King Uzziah before him were seekers of God and the ways of God. As long as they sought God, He made them to prosper. Seek God's way and seek to walk in His ways. There is a world way and there is a word way. Seek the word way and walk in the word. Seek God like one that is thirsty for water. As you thirst for Him you will be filled.

And he sought God in the days of Zechariah, who had understanding in the visions of God: and as long as he sought the LORD, God made him to prosper. -2 Chronicles 26:5

Uzziah the father of Jotham sought God and God made him to prosper. Seek God always. Your success and greatness is tied to you continually seeking him all the days of your life. Seeking God is a life time affair. Seeking God is not a part time endeavor rather it is a full time one. As long as he sought the LORD, God made him to prosper. Seek Him in the morning, in the afternoon and at night. As long as he sought the LORD, He made him to prosper. A branch that is cut off from the plant will not last long. It will wither and die.

The word of God also says we are to study to show ourselves approved. Study to learn more about God and His ways. Acquire more knowledge about the work you do. Go to school if you must. Learn a trade if it is absolutely necessary for your ministry or calling. Get wisdom. Train yourself. Learn what you need to learn. Ignorance is a thief. Ignorance has been stealing and is still stealing from many. Prepare yourself for success and greatness. Prepare mentally, spiritually and even physically. Prepare yourself in every way possible. The level of your preparation is directly related to the level of success you enjoy. Prepare physically also through staying healthy. They say health is wealth. You need to live in health to be able to create wealth.

Prepare by striving to do right always - doing right may not always be easy but doing right is always right. Joseph chose to do right. Live right. Each time you take the right step or do the right thing you move towards achieving or doing more for God. Right in his sight may not be right in the sight of the world but still do the right thing. Prepare your way by walking right. There are Christian believers today who talk one thing and do something else. They talk the talk but do not walk the talk. You are a complete believer when you talk the talk as well as walk the talk. Your daily walk with God prepares you for what He has prepared for you.

Walk with Him through seeking Him in prayer, reading and studying the word of God. Meditate in His word daily. Act or do His word. Grow in faith daily. Some have turned God into a vending machine or ATM. Their relationship with God is what you might call circumstantial. It is only circumstances that draw them to God. When things are rough or tough is the only time you find them praying to God, reading the bible or attending church. In good times they won't pray, study the word or attend fellowship with the brethren. Walking with God is not a part time job. It is a full time job in season and out of season.

How should one prepare his way before God? Prepare by living in humility- he prepared himself by staying humble. Start humble. Continue humble. Finish humble. Humility is a must to excel, succeed and ultimately become great. Uzziah prepared his way before God by being humble. Unfortunately he fell short for when he became strong his heart was lifted up to his own destruction. Start humble and stay humble. Part of preparing for success and greatness is that you are humble always. Little or big, be humble. Small or mighty still remain humble.

But when he was strong, his heart was lifted up to his destruction: for he transgressed against the LORD his God, and went into the temple of the LORD to burn incense upon the altar of incense. -2 Chronicles 26:16

God will prepare you for success and He also expects you to submit to the process of preparation. God will prepare you for what He has prepared for you and He also expects you to prepare yourself for what He has prepared for you. Esther submitted herself to the king's eunuch who prepared her for the throne. She also prepared by submitting to the wise counsel and discipline of her elder cousin and mentor Mordecai. Preparation may not be fun but in the end it is rewarding. Prepare for success and greatness. Allow God to prepare you and be willing to prepare yourself for success and greatness. Jotham became mighty because he prepared his ways before the LORD his God. It is possible for you to become very successful and great but will you pay the price required.

Yes God will prepare you but He does not handle all the preparation. You have a part to play. It is your responsibility to submit to His will for your life. He will not do that for you. It's your responsibility to do the human preparation while God does the divine preparation. He will give you wisdom to write the examination but He will not read for you or write the examination for you. God prepared David but David still needed to ensure that his sling was in proper working order. If it was not, the sling would have let him down when he needed it. God supplied the anointing but David needed to walk in the anointing that God had provided. God put the rod in Moses' hand but God will not use it for him.

Aim to win and succeed in life for that is what you were born to do- win, succeed and be great. Aim to win, prepare to win and work to win. God's plan for your life does not include failure or defeat. Some have settled for failure because they say things like- all fingers are not equal. You were born to succeed and to achieve greatness. Do not settle for less than success and greatness. Do not settle for less than the best that God has planned for you. To win you must aim to win, plan to win and prepare to win. Champions are manifested in the ring or field of play but they are actually made before they enter the battle field. God expects you to prepare to win and He will also prepare you to win. Winners pass through a period or phase of self-preparation. And above all God will prepare you for what He has prepared for you.

Pursue

God said to Gideon- Go in this thy might. Go is an action word. Always, intention without action will not get you any results. Don't sit and wait for manna to drop from heaven. Faith without works is dead. God spoke to Gideon and declared the end from the beginning. He said Gideon would defeat the Midianites long before Gideon had even agreed to take up the responsibility. Even though God had promised him victory, Gideon still had to go out and fight the Midianites. Success does not just happen. You have to make it happen. Don't be lazy. Act on the ideas, dreams and plans you have. It is time to pursue God's vision for your life.

What you don't pursue you won't possess. For the believer in Christ it is a different pattern of pursuit. The unbeliever is pursuing things without pursuing God. Loving even lusting after things but not loving God or the things of God. Loving and pursuing things and sparing no time or place for God. For the believer it is different. Pursue God and He will put His dreams for your life in your heart to pursue.

Delight thyself also in the LORD; and he shall give thee the desires of thine heart. — Psalm 37:4

I say it again because that is what the word of God says. First pursue God then He will put dreams in your heart to pursue. Pursue God and He will give you dreams to pursue. Seek the Giver more than you seek the gifts. God made a promise to Abraham that He would make him a blessed and great nation but first Abraham had to leave his father and mother.

Now the LORD had said unto Abram, Get thee out of thy country, and from thy kindred, and from thy father's house, unto a land that I will shew thee- Genesis 12:1

Don't be deceived for it was not an easy thing to do to leave familiar surroundings, family and friends and go to a place he had not even heard of. But he went anyway and see what God did in his life. Success will cost you your comfort zone. To walk on water Peter had to step out of the boat- *Matthew 14:29*. He was not the only disciple in the boat at the time. God spoke the word and said come but only Peter was bold enough to act on the word. He stepped out in faith and achieved the miraculous. God has been asking you to start that company of yours but you feel secure in that 9 to 5 job of yours even though you hate Monday mornings and don't like your boss. It is time to make plans to pursue God's dream or vision for your life. God said young men shall see visions and old men shall dream dreams.

And it shall come to pass in the last days, saith God, I will pour out of my Spirit upon all flesh: and your sons and your daughters shall prophesy, and your young men shall see visions, and your old men shall dream dreams. - Acts 2:17

When you catch His vision for your life pursue the vision till you succeed and become great. Pursue success till you succeed. Pursue greatness until you achieve greatness. Just make sure that you are succeeding and becoming great on God's purpose for your life. Once Gideon discerned God's assignment for his life he forsook all other things and pursued God's vision for his life.

Too many people are so distracted with trying to make a living that they are not really living. They wake up every day to go to a job they don't like to take orders from a boss they don't like and to earn wages they don't like. They call it earning a living yet what they earn cannot help them make a living. Some work so hard and for so many years that a time comes when the boss or organization lays them off the job in the name of rationalization or restructuring. Don't wait to be restructured or rationalized- whatever that really means. Sack the boss before he/she sacks you and pursue the dreams in your heart while you still have the opportunity. Or while you are still working for the boss give yourself a "night job" (after office hours) of pursuing the dream(s) God has put in your heart. It will take effort but in the end it is worth the effort to chase your own dreams. When you have become strong enough and the dream is unfolding more and more you should then sack the boss and turn the "night job" to your day job.

When God gives you a dream He expects you to pursue it. What you don't pursue you will not possess. Gideon had to accept God's dream for his life and pursue it. Nothing just happens. Stop sitting and waiting for things to happen. Instead go out and make things happen. You cannot succeed by doing nothing. You won't succeed while sitting down and saying you are waiting on God. There is something to do. Start with what you have and from where you are. Pursue your dream. Live your dream.

A woman that is carrying a child in her womb must push or labor to bring forth the child. It is work even hard work but because of the joy of carrying her child she must work to have her baby. To have her baby she must travail. What you are unwilling to pursue you will not possess. To have her baby she must push. She pushes till she brings her baby into the world. You are pregnant with a dream but until you push you will not bring forth your dream.

The first disciples had to pursue God's dream to make them fishers of men. He said to them follow (pursue) me and I will make you fishers of men.

And he saith unto them, Follow me, and I will make you fishers of men. – Matthew 4:19

They left everything and followed Him. It is time to follow (pursue) God's dream for your life. Is your dream worth it?

Then answered Peter and said unto him, Behold, we have forsaken all, and followed thee; what shall we have therefore? – Matthew19:27

Do you believe in your dream? If you do then go ahead and pursue the dream. To catch fish you must go after the fish. To catch the prey the predator must pursue the prey. It is time to pursue your dreams. Pursue that dream to sing, write, be a nurse, engineer, build that orphanage, and invent that piece of equipment. Whatever it is God has put in your heart to do is what you should be pursuing to complete. Pursue your dreams and stop leaving the fulfilment of your dreams to chance. Accomplishing those dreams will not happen by chance as they will only happen by choice. A choice to pursue the dream until it is fulfilled. Pursue God and your God given dreams.

Christ showed Peter a dream or vision that he could walk on water. The Master said to him- come. He had to leave the boat and step out. When he stepped out he found himself walking on water. Your dreams are possible if you will pursue them. Step out of the comfort boat of mediocrity or average and pursue the extraordinary. Don't let fear hinder you. All your dreams are possible but you must pursue them. Peter stepped out at Jesus' command and he accomplished the dream others imagined was impossible. Something is impossible until somebody pursues and accomplishes it. Peter accomplished the impossible because he dared to pursue the dream God gave him.

Jesus spoke to them at once. "Courage!" he said. "It is I, don't be afraid!" Then Peter spoke up. "Lord, if it is really you, order me to come out on the water to you." "Come!" answered Jesus. So Peter got out of the boat and started walking on the water to Jesus. - Matthew 14:27-29 GNT

Step out and go after your dreams. Pursue till you possess your possession or inheritance. Pursue even when you get tired. Gideon was pursuing victory. He and his men got tired at some stage in the pursuit but they did not stop. They refreshed themselves and continued to pursue. They faced obstacles in the course of their pursuit but still they did not stop.

Gideon and his three hundred arrived at the Jordan and crossed over. They were bone-tired but still pressing the pursuit. He asked the men of Succoth, "Please, give me some loaves of bread for my troops I have with me. They're worn out, and I'm hot on the trail of Zebah and Zalmunna, the Midianite kings. - Judges 8:4-5 MSG

Ruth would not give up on her dream to pursue until Naomi's God became her God. Despite strong and persistent efforts to discourage her and get her to drop her pursuit of her dream she would not stop pursuing. She pursued till she possessed her dream.

But Ruth answered, "Don't ask me to leave you! Let me go with you. Wherever you go, I will go; wherever you live, I will live. Your people will be my people, and your God will be my God. Wherever you die, I will die, and that is where I will be buried. May the Lord's worst punishment come upon me if I let anything but death separate me from you!"-Ruth 1:16-17 GNT.

Orpah stopped pursuing and her story stopped there but Ruth did not stop in her pursuit. Her story did not stop. It did not stop until she became very successful and went down in history as someone great. Her story and her life has not been forgotten. How many people remember the name of Orpah today? Very few if any remember her.

Hannah had a dream to have children. She pursued her dream. Her rival mocked her. Her husband tried to discourage her. Still she did not give up her pursuit. She pursued till she took hold of her possession or dream. If you will pursue God's dream for your life you will possess the dream. Don't sit down and wait for your dream to come to you. Rather go after your dream. Stop wasting time and making excuses and go after your dream. Did Hannah possess her dream? Yes she did and with a big bonus from God.

And the Lord visited Hannah, so that she bore three sons and two daughters. And the child Samuel grew before the Lord. - 1 Samuel 2:21 AMP

Look at the birds of the air. God feeds them still they have to go out and gather the provision. God makes the provision available but they must pursue to gather in God's provision for them.

Look at the birds: they do not plant seeds, gather a harvest and put it in barns; yet your Father in heaven takes care of them! Aren't you worth much more than birds? - Matthew 6:26 GNT

Birds don't wait for God to drop the food in their nest. They do not wait for the food to come to them. Rather they go out to where the food is and gather it. Stop waiting for your dream to happen to you rather go out and make your dream happen. Pursue till you possess your God given dream.

Even more so look at the ants and learn from them. Tiny as they are they pursue to possess. They go out to gather food. God provides the supply but tiny as ants are they (the ants) go out to gather God's supply for them.

Go to the ant, you sluggard; consider her ways and be wise! Which, having no chief, overseer, or ruler, provides her food in the summer and gathers her supplies in the harvest. How long will you sleep, O sluggard? When will you arise out of your sleep?-Proverbs 6:6-9 AMP.

David asked God a question. He said- do I pursue. And if I pursue will I overtake and recover all. God said to him- pursue. David pursued and he recovered all.

And David enquired at the LORD, saying, Shall I pursue after this troop? Shall I overtake them? And he answered him, Pursue: for thou shalt surely overtake them, and without fail recover all. – 1 Samuel 30:8

Pursue till you become successful and great. Pursue till you become who God wants you to become and do what God wants you to do. Pursue excellence in life. Pursue holiness. Pursue serving God. Pursue serving your world. Pursue to become better every day. Pursue till you unleash the best of God for your life. Pursue till you fully unleash the warrior-winner in you. Remember there is a winner inside all of us. There is a winner in you. Winners pursue till they win. Pursue till you overcome. Pursue till you become great.

7.7 Patience! Patience! Patience

He who wishes to be rich in a day will be hanged in a year- Da Vinci

We live in a fast paced world. When we want something, we want it now. In fact we want it yesterday. We often pray, yes we do. However we pray today and we want the answer yesterday. If God does not answer we either say He is wasting time or He has failed or does not love us. Understand that greatness takes time. Greatness does not happen instantly. Greatness does not happen overnight. Success does not happen in a day or overnight.

God is committed to your success but He will certainly not give you overnight success. Overnight success stories lack root. And because they lack root they lack the character needed to sustain or maintain success when it arrives. Many overnight successes end up failures, broke, desperate and even dead before their time. Some have won a lottery today and ended up doing drugs and committing suicide tomorrow.

The truly successful are like trees. They spend many years developing tap roots which root them deep. God develops their roots before He grows their stems, leaves and fruits. God will grow your depth before He grows your height. He will root you deep down before raising you high. He does so because you need the depth to sustain the great heights He has prepared for you. Overnight successes are like trees without sufficient depth. Their roots are shallow if any and so they soon fall away during time of testing and challenges. If you are building a sky scraper you spend more time, energy and money building the foundation unlike when you are building a mud house.

Success takes time and you need trailer loads of patience if you want to succeed and become great God's way. Success does not happen in a day rather it happens daily. Between seed time and harvest time is waiting time. Your waiting time is the time to exercise patience. Patience is required particularly when things are slow rather than fast. In fact beware of fast or quick success. What you might call overnight success.

Some seed fell on rocky ground where there wasn't much dirt. That seed grew very fast, because the ground was not deep. - Mark 4:5 NCV

In this particular account of the parable of the sower, the seed grew very fast because the ground was not deep. But as fast as it grew that was how fast it withered away. Overnight success. Not enough root. Not enough depth. Are you worried or fretting that nothing is happening concerning your life? The story right now is that others you know are getting the breakthrough but you are not. All your friends are married but you are not. Most of the people you know have their own children but you do not. Envy not. Fret not if you do not have yours yet. God is spending time to develop your roots and dig you deep.

God will develop character or strength in you first before He gives you the miracle for you need character to keep the blessing. You don't want to get the blessing today and tomorrow it is gone. God does not want you to reign briefly. He wants you to reign a long time. You don't want to be called- he/she used to be successful, rich, married, blessed. No you don't and even more God does not want that for you.

Waiting is not fun but it has its rewards or benefits. When you are waiting it always looks like you have waited too long. Waiting is painful but it has its rewards especially if you are waiting for the promise keeper. The One who never fails. The One who keeps covenant to a thousand generations.

He hath remembered his covenant forever, the word which he commanded to a thousand generations. - Psalm 105:8

This God cannot lie and He does not lie. He is not weak. He is strong, able, dependable and capable. If His word promised it His hand will do it. If the promise is in His word, He will do it. It looks like you are waiting forever and the promise or promises have failed. His promises never fail. He does not forget His promise. What He said He will do, He will do. Remember all His promises are yes and amen- so be it.

For all the promises of God in him are yea, and in him Amen, unto the glory of God by us. - 2 Corinthians1:20

Ruth had to wait for her throne. Joseph had to be patient for his time and his throne. Jesus endured the cross to get to his throne. David was anointed one day but did not get to the throne the same day. He had to wait for his time and his throne. Patience is a must if you must reach greatness for greatness is progressive and does not happen instantly. Greatness is not like instant coffee or noodles. It is not fast food. If Jesus who was God had to wait, then who are you not to wait? If you want God's best you must be willing to wait. And remember you can't help God fulfil His promise. Abraham and Sarah tried to help God and today the world is still living with the consequences of their trying to help God.

We are called to be followers of those who through faith and patience inherited the promise of God. You have need of patience. The palm tree is patient as such it grows highest among all trees. You need patience, patience, patience and patience.

For ye have need of patience, that, after ye have done the will of God, ye might receive the promise. -Hebrews 10:36 KJV

Success that is godly and enduring happens little by little. Like growth it happens daily and not in a day. It does not happen overnight instead it happens little by little. It will not happen in an instant but if you trust God and wait for Him to prosper you He will.

Da Vinci said and I quote- "He who wishes to be rich in a day will be hanged in a year". True. Many are desperate to succeed yet not desperate to wait to succeed. We want to succeed today but we want that success to happen yesterday. So desperate that some would even do anything to succeed.

To succeed you must wait to succeed. If you want to succeed God's way you need to wait. Anything worth having is worth waiting for. Waiting is not fun for the flesh but it is worth it in the end. Get it quick and you might lose it in the end. True success will not happen in a flash or an instant. It will not happen overnight or in the twinkling of an eye. Well the truth is you can achieve instant success but it will not last. It's about the roots. To go high you must root deep. To climb higher you must root deeper. As high as you want to go is how deep you must sink your roots in God.

Right now it looks like nothing is happening in your life. Don't worry for God is digging your roots deep. He is developing you from the inside to the outside. Your roots are first spiritual before they are physical. God is building or growing you up for the inheritance He has prepared for you. You won't lose your inheritance and that is why God is growing you up to be able to handle the inheritance when it comes. Your success may not happen in a flash but it will happen little by little. You will succeed but little by little until you become very successful and great.

Little by little I will drive them out from before you, until you have increased and are numerous enough to take possession of the land. - Exodus 23:30AMP

Scriptures say that we should be followers of those who through faith and patience obtained the promise. Patience is a necessary companion of faith. Add patience to your faith. Lack of patience can lead to mistakes and compromise. Don't be tired of waiting for God to help you. Don't be intimidated by the delay you are experiencing. If God has promised it He will perform what He has promised. But you have need of patience. Impatience has consequences but patience has reward.

Many of the children of Israel that came out of Egypt did not make it to the Promised Land because they were a grumbling, complaining and impatient bunch. What God said He will do He will do. It may happen soon or it may happen later but it will happen. Sooner or later God will fulfil His promise to you. But you must be patient. Impatience cost many of the children of Israel their promised land. Impatience cost Elimelech and his children their lives. Impatience will cause you to make the wrong choices. It will make you compromise and adopt ways that are not necessarily the way of God. And when you adopt such ways the fruit or end result will cause you pain even loss.

Patience is a very important element of your faith walk. If you want what God has planned and prepared for you then you ought to patiently wait for Him. To walk with God you must walk patiently. Even when you can't see the way out you should patiently trust Him. Don't try to help Him. You are too small to help God and God did not ask for your help. To see the work of God manifested in your life you must be patient. Patience is hard for the flesh but the fruit of impatience can be bitter later on.

Patiently wait for God to bring His best for you and out of you. Patiently wait for Him to unleash success and greatness from inside you. Jesus patiently waited for 30 years to have a successful and great 3 year ministry that is still being celebrated. Patiently wait for your turn. David had to patiently wait to get to the throne. He did not get to the throne the same day he was anointed king. God gave Joseph a dream but he did not wake up the next day to find that the dream had happened. He had to be patient and he was patient. Be patient with God and be patient with you. You need patience. Patience! Patience! Patience! You must have patience if you want to succeed and become great.

7.8 Persist till you win

Persistence beats resistance- Rick Warren

Your dream will be tested. So persist till you birth that dream God has given you. Persist till you win. Winners win and winning is what winners do. To win however you must persist till you win. You may not win or succeed at the first attempt or even the ninth attempt but don't quit till you win. You quit you lose. If you don't quit you will win. We are born to win. We are born to conquer for we are more than conquerors through Christ that loves us. We are warrior-winners.

Defeat is temporary not permanent. What makes defeat permanent is when you allow the failed attempts stop you from trying. God had told Isaac to stay in Gerar and he stayed but prosperity or success did not happen immediately. He faced opposition and had frustration.

And he removed from thence, and digged another well; and for that they strove not: and he called the name of it Rehoboth; and he said, for now the LORD hath made room for us, and we shall be fruitful in the land. -Genesis 26:22

Isaac had suffered disappointment, setback and discouragement. Everything that could go wrong had gone wrong. He had done all he knew to do. Yet it seemed success had eluded him. Life will sometimes throw setbacks, disappointments and discouragement at you. What you do when such times come is critical to success. Do you allow your setbacks and the like to stop you? Or do you keep pressing on. God had instructed him to stay in that land. You would have expected that because he was in the "will of God" for his life, everything should go according to plan and there should be no opposition or disappointments. But remember that the land which had milk and honey also had giants.

Isaac faced the giants of discouragement, disappointment and setback. But he conquered them. How? He did not quit when the easiest thing to do was quit. He dug again and again and again till God made room for him.

To succeed or achieve anything worthwhile or significant you must persist till you win. You are not going to get something for nothing. To win in life you must be bold, strong, courageous and have a never say die attitude. An attitude or disposition that never gives up. An old cliché has it that "if you try the first time and you don't succeed, try again".

Winners don't quit till they have won. Isaac had God on his side. He was in that land because God told him to stay in the land. God on your side does not make you immune to challenges and obstacles. God on your side however guarantees that you will triumph or overcome challenges and obstacles. You have to "fight" to possess your possession. It's a fight of faith. And in this fight

God is committed to you winning. But you must be courageous and persist till you win.

Don't quit. Don't turn back. Don't give up. Yes there are obstacles and some are so large it looks like you will not reach the Promised Land. It looks like the more you try to make things work, the more things are not working. Many times Isaac dug wells and many times the opposition stopped his wells. But he could not be stopped. He dug again. He kept digging. Finally God made room for Isaac. I see God making room for you. It's always too early to quit. If God has not quit, surely you should not quit.

Yes you may have submitted many job applications without success. Dig again. Submit another. God will make room for you if you don't stop digging or trying. You may have tried many times to have that baby and still not had one. Dig again. Try again and God will make room for you. Tried your hands at making that home work but ended up frustrated. Dig again. God will make room for you. You have prayed for that breakthrough yet the breakthrough has not come. Dig again. Pray again. God will make room for you. You may have tried many times and failed. Dig again. Try again. God will make room for you. Failures are people that would have succeeded but they quit just before they succeeded.

Be like Isaac. Be a finisher. If you hold on till the end you will win. Persist till you win. God is with you, for you and in you. So power, grace and anointing to succeed is on your side. Winners are people who refused to quit and because they refused to quit on their dreams and expectations, God made room for them. If you do not let your setbacks stop you, God will prepare a comeback for you. If you do not let the disappointments stop you, God will set you up for an appointment with success. But you must dig again. Dig again and God will make room for you.

The word of God also says that the righteous may fall seven times but they rise again. Winners may fall but they don't stay down. They get up and go again. In fact they keep going till they win.

Even if good people fall seven times, they will get back up. But when trouble strikes the wicked, that's the end of them. – Proverbs 24:16 CEV

A knock down is not a knock out until you refuse to get up. If you can get up after you are knocked down you will win. To persist means to hang in there until you win. There was a woman who had an issue of blood for twelve years. For twelve years she went everywhere looking for healing but she did not get it. Doctors had told her to forget healing. There is no way she can get healed but her faith would not let her give up. As long as your faith says yes God won't say no. And certainly what men or the devil think does not matter when your faith and your God says yes. Her faith said yes and God said yes too and her healing was settled.

And a woman having an issue of blood twelve years, which had spent all her living upon physicians, neither could be healed of any. Came behind him, and touched the border of his garment: and immediátely her issue of blood stanched. – Luke 8:43-44

Moses kept going to Pharaoh and telling him- thus says the LORD, let my people go that they might serve me. For a while pharaoh would not let the people go. The more Moses requested the more Pharaoh refused and would not let the people go. The more Moses asked the more it looked like nothing was happening. In fact things got worse. Even after several plagues pharaoh would still not let Israel go. Still God would not let Moses give up. Encouraged by God Moses did not give up. Moses persisted and in the end Pharaoh released Israel. Moses persisted and won in the end. Failures quit before they have won while winners quit after they have won. Moses was a winner and he did not quit until he won.

He called for Moses and Aaron by night, and said, Rise up, get out from among my people, both you and the Israelites; and go, serve the Lord, as you said. Also take your flocks and your herds, as you have said, and be gone! And [ask your God to] bless me also. - Exodus 12:31-32 AMP.

If you are in Christ you are born a winner but to win you must "fight". Life will not give you what you desire rather life will give you what God has prepared for you and that you fight to take. To win in life you must fight to win. To win you must persist till you win. Yes, you have prayed and prayed still the answer to the prayer has not happened. Persist- stay at it till the answer comes. It's always too early to give up if you have God and are pursuing His plan for your life. It looks like the more you pray the worse things have got. That was

Moses's experience. Don't quit. Persist by faith for soon what you have been praying and believe to happen will happen.

Winners win and all those that are in Christ are born to win. You are fighting to win but all those and the things fighting you are fighting to lose. Things look bad naturally but you are headed for victory. Things look like they have not improved even though you have been praying. Persist and keep faith in God. There is more happening that you can't see so persist till you win. God can't lose and because you are on God's side you can't lose. Things look slow or even stagnant yet you are on your way to winning. Moses did not quit. In the end he got his desire. Don't quit. If you quit you lose but if you don't quit you will end up winning. So persist till you win. You are not there yet but persist till you become everything that God wants you to become and you do everything God wants you to do.

That woman with the issue of blood persisted till she got her healing. Twelve years did not weaken her resolve or courage to get healed. She persisted and she won. There will be delays, disappointments, setbacks and the like. Those things can't stop you except you permit them to stop you. If you will persist you will win. Joseph persisted with his God given dream. He went through all kinds of trouble but he would not let go of his dream. If you don't let go of your dream your dream won't let go of you. Dreams happen and God's dream for you will happen. Dream success and greatness and God will cause it to happen in your life. Persist till you succeed. You will succeed. Persist till you become great. God will make you successful and great.

8

TEAR THE LEASH AND MOVE FORWARD

If you want to fly, you have to give up the stuff that weighs you down. – David Roads

Remember the baby elephant? If only it knew that it could rip up the chain and the stake that held it down in one place it would be free to fulfill its potential as an elephant. An eagle that has been set free will still not fly if it does not know that it has been set free. Your case is however different because now you know. The "chains" that have held you back will no longer hold you back. Every chain that has held you down from moving into your destiny and purpose in God is broken. You can move forward, upward and ahead in life.

What is a leash? Something that holds a thing down. A chain can hold a lion down. Do you know what keeps a ship down? Something "small" called an anchor. Looks small but it is able to keep a ship down. What is it that keeps a door or gate shut? A tiny thing- (tiny in comparison to the gate) called a lock. What is it that holds a car even a truck down? It's a tiny lever called an emergency brake. What kept the BIG elephant down, limited and unable to move forward is a SMALL chain and stake or peg.

What is the leash that has kept you down and kept you from success? Gideon had some leashes keeping him down. A time came and God helped him to remove the leashes and he went forward till he became successful and great. What is keeping you down and unable to move forward? This is your time to tear down the leashes for it is your turn to become successful and great. It's your turn to unleash the winner in you. Deal with these things. You can't permit these things to keep you tied down anymore. Remove the leash for it is time to unleash the warrior in you. Unleash the warrior-winner in you. Remove every leash that is stopping you from succeeding and becoming great. Tear the leash.

8.1 Fear

It's been said before and I say it again. Fear is an enemy. Kill fear before fear kills your dream. Fear does not come from God. It comes from the devil. Kill fear with faith. Faith is not negotiable if you must become all that God has planned for you. It is commonly said that the fear of failure is worse than failure itself. Fear limited Gideon.

And there came an angel of the LORD, and sat under an oak which was in Ophrah, that pertained unto Joash the Abiezrite: and his son Gideon threshed wheat by the winepress, to hide it from the Midianites. - Judges 6:11

A warrior-winner hiding from what is afraid of him. Hiding from what God has given him power to deal with. It's time to kill fear. Fear of failing will no longer be able to stop you from doing what God wants you to do. It is time to rise above your fears and step out in faith. Fear is not from God rather it is from the devil. That is why Christ would always say fear not. Kill fear by doing the good that you are afraid to do. Leave that paid employment and start your own business. They call it job security. Indeed! Beat fear by doing what you are afraid to do. Pursue that dream that you are afraid to pursue. You need courage. Someone has said that courage is not the absence of fear. Rather courage is the ability to do what you have to do even when you are afraid.

If you must experience the supernatural you must defeat fear. Beat fear and achieve the impossible. A certain woman was down to her last meal and she told the prophet she and her child were simply going to go ahead and eat that last meal and die. Then the prophet asked her to give that last meal to him. Sounds wicked but what does she have to lose. She gave out the meal and that singular step gave her the breakthrough she needed. She beat fear when she gave her last.

And Elijah said unto her, Fear not; go and do as thou hast said: but make me thereof a little cake first, and bring it unto me, and after make for thee and for thy son. - 1 Kings17:13

You too can beat fear by doing what the enemy has been using fear to discourage you from doing. Perhaps you are in an abusive relationship that you know is no good for you. You refuse to come out of the relationship because the voice in your head is telling you that if you let him or her go you will not find another person. That is fear speaking. Dare your fear and quit the relationship. Fear is a liar and has been lying to you. Believe the lies no more. That limiting or binding fear that keeps you from doing the good that you should do is not from God

For God hath not given us the spirit of fear; but of power, and of love, and of a sound mind. – 2Timothy 1:7

Fear has been speaking to you that you will soon die. It's a lie for the word of God says God will satisfy you with long life- *Psalm 91:16*. Fear has been telling you that your disease is incurable. It's a lie for the word of God in *1 Peter 2:24* says by His stripes all sickness and disease was nailed to the cross and you have been healed- past tense. Your healing was paid for on the cross so you can live in health all the days of your life. Fear said you are barren because you have been married 10 years now and have no children. It's a lie. The word of God says nothing shall be barren in your land- *Exodus 23:26*.

Dearly beloved that is why you need faith. Fear only thrives where there is no faith. Fear only rules when faith is on leave. Darkness is king when light is asleep. Faith will kill fear any day and anytime. And like somebody said whenever fear knocks on your door let faith open the door. It's time to step out of fear mode and step into faith mode. Peter stepped out of the boat and walked on water. He killed fear when he stepped out of the boat and walked on water. He did the miraculous when he stepped out in faith.

And he said, Come. And when Peter was come down out of the ship, he walked on the water, to go to Jesus. – Matthew 14:29

When Gideon heard the word of God fear disappeared and the same Midianites he was afraid of he was able to defeat. Fear not. Don't be afraid to step out and become everything God wants you to become. You can be everything God wants you to be and you certainly can do everything God planned for you to do. However tear down the leash or chain called fear.

8. 2. Procrastination

One dictionary definition for the word procrastinate is to postpone doing what one should be doing. In another place it has been defined as postpone or delay needlessly. Procrastination for me is any proclamation or action (or inaction) that delays your arrival at your destination, dream, goal or target. Have you ever found yourself saying- tomorrow I will do it only to get to tomorrow and you still have not done it. Well I have.

Procrastination delays even kills dreams. We procrastinate when we don't take action on our dreams. You stand still. You have the potential for more but you are standing still because you are still procrastinating. We wait for perfect conditions before taking action and the word of God says there will never be a time when you will have perfect conditions for doing the good you must do. If you wait for perfect conditions you will wait forever.

He who observes the wind (and waits for all conditions to be favorable) will not sow, and he who regards the clouds will not reap- Ecclesiastes 11:4 AMP.

Waiting for perfect conditions to do what you must do will cause you to wait forever. I once heard someone say that procrastination is a thief of time. I will do it tomorrow and tomorrow never comes because when tomorrow turns to today we still say tomorrow I will do. Tomorrow, tomorrow, tomorrow. I will do it tomorrow. Write that book tomorrow. Get that education tomorrow. Forgive my husband tomorrow. Accept salvation tomorrow. Still we never come round to doing what we said yesterday that we would do today. Whatever your hands find to do just do it. What you have is today. Only God guarantees tomorrow. Procrastination is one leash you need to tear off yourself.

Procrastination kills dreams. It delays even denies you success. Make the most of every day. Plan for tomorrow but make the most of each day God gives you. Make the most of each day by doing something that will bless you and bless somebody else. Kill procrastination by taking active meaningful steps towards your dream. Make sure you improve daily. Learn something new. Meditate on the word of God. God's word is medicine for all thy flesh. Make sure you are not standing still. Make sure you are growing, getting better, doing better. Improve yourself daily. The best medicine or antidote for procrastination is positive action towards your dream. Make sure you are not standing still and doing nothing. A couple of lepers found themselves procrastinating their next decision and thus delaying their breakthrough. Off cause they stood still. One day they spoke to each other and removed the leash called procrastination.

And there were four leprous men at the entering in of the gate: and they said one to another, why sit we here until we die? If we say, we will enter into the city, then the famine is in the city, and we shall die there: and if we sit still here, we die also. Now therefore come, and let us fall unto the host of the Syrians: if they save us alive, we shall live; and if they kill us, we shall but die. And they rose up in the twilight, to go unto the camp of the Syrians: and when they were come to the uttermost part of the camp of Syria, behold, there was no man there. - 2Kings 7:3- 5

Kill procrastination with positive action. They said to themselves- why sit we here and die? As long as they were doubtful and procrastinating the next step they remained stagnant. When they took action God gave them a miracle that was beyond anything they had imagined. They took one step and God did the rest. God has been waiting for you to take that step of faith and He will surprise you with a breakthrough beyond your imagination.

Be like these lepers and take a step. You have stalled enough. Arise and take action on your dreams and ideas. You have sat in one place too long because you have been waiting for something to happen. Now it is time for you to make something happen. Move and you will see what God will do in your life. Kill procrastination by taking action on your dreams. Start that business or company. Learn that skill. Grow that ability you have. Release those songs that God has put inside you. Start to take action towards building that shopping mall. Why rent a space in the mall when you can own the mall? Get tired of being an employee and start to take concrete steps towards becoming an employer. It is more blessed to be an employer than an employee. Don't spend all your life as an employee when God wants you to be an employer.

Don't wait for perfect conditions before executing the dreams of success and greatness God planted inside you. Don't let those dreams die inside you. Stop procrastinating and waiting for tomorrow. Like the shoe manufacturer Nike would say- Just do it. And scriptures also say whatever your hands find do it with all thy might. Success and greatness is waiting to be unleashed from inside you. Procrastinate no more. Tear the leash called procrastination today.

8.3. Excuses

As human beings we have been trained in the art of using excuses, but today I want you to write on your mirror, "no more excuses, get up and do it- Cindy Trimm

In the beginning Adam failed and when he was asked, he made excuses. Today the world is still making excuses for failure. Men have not stopped making excuses since Adam and Eve fell in Eden. Adam made excuses then and man is still making excuses today. We make many excuses for mediocrity and failure and they keep us down, limited and restricted. What are some of the excuses you have been using to stop your own rise, progress and achievement in life? What excuses are you using to keep you down and limited?

God called Moses and this is what Moses said to God:

And Moses answered and said, but, behold, they will not believe me, nor hearken unto my voice: for they will say, The LORD hath not appeared unto thee. - Exodus 4:1

1st excuse- they will not believe me.

Really. God will never send you to do something He has not already equipped you to do. God gives you an idea for a book and you say nobody will buy the book. Who told you so? Sing that song and you say nobody will buy the album CD. Who told you? He gives you a business idea to take to the market place. You are afraid and say nobody will patronize you. Nobody will believe me. Nobody will help me. Nobody will give me. Nobody will support me. How many times have you said that and who told you. Who God appoints He also anoints. If He has told you to do something He has also already provided the ability to do it. Fight the negative thoughts that cause doubt and breed low self-esteem. Instead of making excuses and saying nobody likes me begin to tell yourself I am highly favored because God is with me.

And the angel came in unto her, and said, Hail, thou that art highly favoured, the Lord is with thee: blessed art thou among women. – Luke 1:28

Believe in God. Believe in yourself. Believe in His dream and plan for your life. If He sent you there you will succeed. If he gave you the idea surely He has already prepared the market for that idea. If He gives you a song He has also prepared those who will listen to and be blessed by the song. If He puts a message in your heart it is because there is someone waiting to hear and be blessed by the message. Don't imagine everybody will like you or buy your product or patronize your service. In the same manner don't imagine that nobody likes you. Still your product or service will find room in the world. You can do what God says you can do and you can be everything He says you can be.

2nd excuse- I am not able

And Moses said unto the LORD, O my Lord, I am not eloquent, neither heretofore, nor since thou hast spoken unto thy servant: but I am slow of speech, and of a slow tongue. – Exodus 4:10

Inabilities? No one has everything but everyone has something. There are no useless persons in life. God is too good to create thrash or nonsense. And that is why it is an insult to God to describe any human as useless, stupid, foolish, without future ambition, nonsense or good for nothing. God created everyone with potential to be successful and great. He is a good God and he created all humans to achieve success and greatness. Men fail when they refuse to cooperate with the creator God, live for Him, love Him and walk in His ways.

Men become less than great because they ignore God and ignore the potential that He put in them. Some might even touch or scratch the surface of the depths of success He planned for them but still they do not reach their full potential. Hear the confession of Gideon- I am the least. What did Moses say? I can't talk well. Inabilities? All of us have them. Abilities? We all have them too. Some have one others have more but everybody has something. All your inabilities cannot stop you except you permit it. Our lives are a mix of abilities and inabilities, strengths and weaknesses, things we can do and things we can't do and things we are good at and things we are not good at. Only God is good at all things good. Only God is perfect. Only God is strong. Only God is almighty.

God is the only one who never sleeps nor slumbers. He is creator and He never tires, gets weary or gets weak. Men fail because they concentrate on their weaknesses instead of their strengths. They ignore their abilities while focusing on their inabilities. They don't develop their skills, abilities and strength because they are focused on their inabilities, weakness and what they don't have. Still we all are blessed with ability or abilities. God gave to every man ability.

And unto one he gave five talents, to another two, and to another one; to every man according to his several ability; and straightway took his journey. - Matthew 25:15

Failure happens when we ignore our abilities and concentrate on our inabilities. Moses pointed to everything that was wrong with him and ignored everything that was right about him. Hear him- I stammer, I am not eloquent. We all have strengths and weaknesses. Yes we have abilities and inabilities. Your one ability, if that is all that you have can make room for you in life. That is because the gift of a man makes way for him and brings him before great men- *Proverbs 18:16*. The scripture did not say gifts rather it says the gift of a man- singular makes room for him

A man's gift maketh room for him, and bringeth him before great men. – Proverbs 18:16

The problem with humans is not lack of gift or talent or ability rather it is a problem of ignoring what we have. We so to say major on our inabilities and minor on our abilities. The problem the man with the one talent in Matthew 25 was that he buried or hid his talent.

But he that had received one went and digged in the earth, and hid his lord's money. -Matthew 25:18

One talent or ability is enough for you to succeed and achieve greatness. Why worry that you can't sing when you have the ability to preach. You lack ability to teach but you have ability to make people laugh. Concentrate on what you can do and ignore what you cannot do. What you can't do you can't do. What you can do you can do if you give attention to it. Your many inabilities cannot stop your one or two abilities. God gave you ability that is enough to prosper you. You have more than enough of what you need to prosper, succeed and be great. So do not let your inabilities stop you. You have enough ability to succeed and be great in life. And that is why the LORD said to Gideon:

And the LORD looked upon him, and said, go in this thy might, and thou shalt save Israel from the hand of the Midianites: have not I sent thee? – Judges 6:14

There is enough might (ability) to start and complete God's assignment for your life. So do not be distracted by your inabilities. Enough might is inside you and with God almighty you can become all that God wants you to become. So go in this thy might and unleash the warrior-winner in you. Remove the leash men including you have put on you that is holding you down. Break free from your perceived limitations. Excuse yourself from the excuses you have used to limit yourself up till now.

Many are still making excuses why they cannot go ahead and achieve or succeed. I am not educated. My background. I am poor. I am short in height. The economy is bad. The government is not favorable. Nobody likes me. I could go on and on. Excuses slow you down and eventually paralyze you. One wise man said excuses are the blocks found in the house of failure. Excuses produce so much negative energy that stalls your faith, courage and progress.

Let us turn from making excuses. Let us motivate ourselves and others to action. I will make it. I can do all things through Christ who strengthens me. I am fearfully and wonderfully made. Anything is possible for me because I believe. God is on my side so nothing shall be impossible for me. I will not fear what man can do to me because God is with me. The Lord is my strength. He is my shepherd and so I shall not want. God has to be your chief motivator and the bible has to be your number one motivational or inspiration for success. Fill your mind and spirit every day with the word of God and fear, anxiety, discouragement, negativity and darkness will have no place in your life.

Achievers or winners give reasons why they can succeed rather than make excuses why they cannot succeed. You are born to win and you will win if you choose to win. Get rid of all the excuses you have been using to stop you. Remove the leash and unleash that winner in you.

3ʳᵈ **excuse- my background**

Gideon complained about his background. Hear him

And he said unto him, Oh my Lord, wherewith shall I save Israel? Behold, my family is poor in Manasseh, and I am the least in my father's house. – Judges 6:15

Your past cannot stop your future. Your mistakes can't stop what God wants to do in your life. God is bigger than your mistakes or sins once you have repented and forsaken them. Who your parents were or are is not enough to stop God's plan for your life. He did not make a mistake to have caused you to come from that family of yours. Gideon said- my family is the least and in my family I am the least. My father did not send me to formal school. Well I have news for you. The early apostles were unschooled and were mere fishermen but see what God did in them and with them. From uneducated fishermen to world champions. What a turnaround.

Now when they saw the boldness of Peter and John, and perceived that they were unlearned and ignorant men, they marveled; and they took knowledge of them, that they had been with Jesus. – Acts 4:13

They were unlearned and ignorant but they had been with Jesus Christ and He made the difference in their life. When God is with you He will make the difference in your life. Even Jesus himself began life as a carpenter's son. Not what you might call a privileged background. To start with He was born in a manger- a place where they kept sheep. So if you like He was not born with the proverbial silver spoon in His mouth. Where you were born cannot stop you from reaching where God has planned for you. Your past cannot stop the future for better is the end of a matter than the beginning.

Though thy beginning was small, yet thy latter end should greatly increase. – Job 8:7

You were not in a position to choose your background so why worry about your background. Where you are going to is far more important than where you have been or where you are coming from. Who you were cannot stop who you will be. Your background can't stop you and you are on your way to becoming that person God planned that you will become.

What has been holding you back and stopping you from moving forward. Maybe it is your past. You made mistakes in the past and the enemy has convinced you that those mistakes are stopping your rising or going forward. I lose you from that past in Jesus name. Your past does not have the power to stop your future or your destiny. Untie yourself from the past and unleash the power of God inside you. You are blessed of God and it is time to unleash the kingdom of God from within you. Tear yourself lose from every excuse. It is your season to unleash the warrior or winner in you.

4ᵗʰ excuse- *I don't have connections*

When Jesus saw him lie, and knew that he had been now a long time in that case, he saith unto him, Wilt thou be made whole? The impotent man answered him, Sir, I have no man, when the water is troubled, to put me into the pool: but while I am coming, another steppeth down before me. - John 5:6-7

Jesus asked the impotent man a question. Do you want to be made whole? He answered with excuses just like many are doing today. His first excuse was that he has no man to help him. He was saying I have no connections. There are those that believe that they can't find money, a job or opportunities because they have no connections. They go around looking for who will give them an introductory note to some high ranking person so that they can get favors. For thirty eight years this impotent man had been looking for "connections" and still had neither found the connections nor been made whole.

Like this man you have been looking in the wrong places and with the wrong people. Many abandon their country of birth in search of green pastures without taking the time to follow God's plan for their lives. Only for them to migrate to some foreign land and end up with brown pasture or no pasture at all. Let the LORD be your source and guide (shepherd) and you will not lack green pasture for:

He maketh me to lie down in green pastures: he leadeth me beside the still waters. - Psalm 23:2

Acknowledge God as your source and He will connect you to the channels (men) that matter for your lifting and promotion. You don't need everybody but when you acknowledge God as your source He will bring you in touch with those that are important to your rising in life. It was God that connected the butler with Joseph. The most important connection you need is a connection to the source- God not a connection to the channels- men. Channels will fail but the source will never fail. That is why we are told to seek first the kingdom of God and all these other things will be added unto you.

5th excuse- My age

I answered, "Sovereign LORD, I don't know how to speak; I am too young."- Jeremiah 1:6 GNT

I am too young! People say to you that you are too young! Some place limitations on themselves by telling themselves they are too young. For some, other people place limitations on them by telling them they are too young. Listen to the prophet Jeremiah. He said- I am too young.

Then said I, Ah, Lord GOD! behold, I cannot speak: for I am a child. – Jeremiah 1 :6

Youth should not be a barrier to your doing what God has called you to do. David was a youth when he defeated Goliath. In the same place the older people failed youthful David succeeded. Youth has its own advantage. Youth are more adventurous and bold to take risks by faith while older folk are over cautious even fearful. Even Jesus said except you become like a little child you cannot enter the kingdom of heaven. Youth is not an obstacle except you permit it. Josiah was only eight years old when he began to reign

Josiah was eight years old when he began to reign, and he reigned thirty and one years in Jerusalem. And his mother's name was Jedidah, the daughter of Adaiah of Boscath.- 2Kings 22:1.

Who said you are too young? God has used young people in the past and is still using young people to do great things. At age 12 Jesus Christ was discussing the scriptures with teachers and doctors of the law.

And it came to pass, that after three days they found him in the temple, sitting in the midst of the doctors, both hearing them, and asking them questions. And all that heard him were astonished at his understanding and answers. – Luke 2:46-47

Don't allow anybody put a tag or label on you that you are too young. You are not too young to have dreams of your own and see them fulfilled. God gave Joseph a dream of where He was taking him at a very young age. Who said you are too young? God also declared that He will rain His anointing on youths and give them visions.

And it shall come to pass in the last days, saith God, I will pour out of my Spirit upon all flesh: and your sons and your daughters shall prophesy, and your young men shall see visions, and your old men shall dream dreams: - Acts 2:17

It says young men shall see visions. God will pour out of His Spirit on all flesh and young men (including women) shall see visions. If God calls you then you are not too young. Samuel learned to hear the voice of God at a young age. He started to serve God at a young age. No wonder the preacher in Ecclesiastes advises that we should serve the creator in the days of our youth

Remember now thy Creator in the days of thy youth, while the evil days come not, nor the years draw nigh, when thou shalt say, I have no pleasure in them- Ecclesiastes 12:1

How old was Jesus Christ when He started His earthly ministry. He was 33 years old. Daniel, Shadrach, Meshach and Abednego were all young men. Ruth and Esther were all young women. Age is a number not an obstacle. Age should not stop you. I have heard people say that they want to work as employees for 65 years of their life, retire from paid employment and give God the remnant of their years. How many more years and how much strength do you still have after 65 years to give to God? Who told you that God deserves or wants the remnant? You spend your best years and strength for Caesar then you give God the lesser part of your years. God deserves your best not your worst. Don't wait to reach old age before giving God your best.

However on the other hand you also find some making excuses that they are too old or they allow others put a leash or a cap on what they can do by telling them they are too old. You are too young is as bad as you are too old. Again age is not a barrier. After all God promised to anoint the old and that old men shall dream dreams. You are not too old to do exploits for God

And it shall come to pass in the last days, saith God, I will pour out of my Spirit upon all flesh: and your sons and your daughters shall prophesy, and your young men shall see visions, and your old men shall dream dreams: - Acts 2:17

God entered into a covenant with Abraham when he was 75 years old. At that age many would have since retired and be waiting to die. Abraham at age 100 and his wife Sarah at age 90 had a child. God gave them laughter (Isaac). I prophesy that God will give you laughter. Men have told you that you are too old to get married. Ignore them. Ignore your age. Your age can't limit you except you allow it. God will give you laughter. Yes you have been married for 10 years and still don't have children and the devil is lying to you that all hope is lost.

With God hope is not lost for you and you will yet carry your own children. At age 85, Caleb was still uprooting mountains and conquering obstacles. He was not afraid or too old to face challenges and conquer them. Yet he was 85 years old. At age 85 Caleb was still winning "titles" and living the life of a champion. Who told you that you are too old?

Joshua, it was forty-five years ago that the LORD told Moses to make that promise, and now I am eighty-five. Even though Israel has moved from place to place in the desert, the LORD has kept me alive all this time as he said he would. I'm just as strong today as I was then, and I can still fight as well in battle. So I'm asking you for the hill country that the LORD promised me that day. You were there. You heard the other spies talk about that part of the hill country and the large, walled towns where the Anakim live. But maybe the LORD will help me take their land, just as he promised. – Joshua 14:10- 12 CEV

He is eighty five and he is neither retired nor tired. He said give me this mountain for if the LORD is with me I will conquer it. I will drive out the opposition as long as the LORD is with me. Age did not affect his faith. His age did not dampen or kill his faith in God. How old was Moses when God sent him to go bring Israel out of Egypt? He was 80 years old.

At the time when they spoke to the king, Moses was eighty years old, and Aaron was eighty-three. – Exodus 7:7

Zechariah and Elizabeth the parents of John the Baptist were old and past child bearing age but see what God did for them. He gave them a miracle when the world had written them off that they were too old to have children. God will give you the miracle you have waited for even though you are past the age in the eyes of the world.

Old men shall dream dreams. You can still get that education or degree. Recently the story was told of a woman who got a PhD degree at age 102. Ingeborg Rapoport completed her medical studies and wrote her PhD thesis in 1937. At that time because of oppression by the Nazi's she was denied the opportunity to take the final oral exams that would have led to her being awarded the degree. Nearly eighty years later in 2015 it was reported that professors from the faculty of Medicine at Hamburg University travelled to examine her in Berlin. She passed the exam and received the PhD degree that was denied her nearly seven decades ago. And she was 102 years old. Who said age is a barrier or obstacle? It is only when you permit it that your age can stop you. You can still unleash the best of God for your life irrespective of your age.

Tear every self-imposed or people imposed leash that has kept you down and unable to reach your best and your highest in God. It is time to unleash success and greatness. It is time to unleash the warrior in you. It is your season to move forward, upward and ahead in life but don't accommodate or tolerate any limitations or restrictions that God did not put on you. Let God alone set the boundaries of your life. If God is not stopping you let nothing and no one stop you. Go ahead and be everything God planned for you to become. Go ahead and succeed beyond your imagination.

9

TO GOD BE THE GLORY

---

*Keep your head up in failure and your head
down in success. - Jerry Seinfeld*

Before you succeed stay humble. Even more after you succeed stay humble.
Pride happens before a fall. Going up may be hard but coming down is
comparatively easier. It might take someone five years to build a skyscraper but
within a couple of minutes the same building can be pulled down. Building up
is hard but pulling down is easy. God told Israel after you have eaten and are
full be careful lest you forget that it is God that gives you power to succeed.

*But thou shalt remember the LORD thy God: for it is he that giveth thee power to
get wealth that he may establish his covenant which he sware unto thy fathers, as
it is this day. – Deuteronomy 8:18*

As you succeed and move towards greatness you must learn to stay humble.
Rising high in life requires that you still keep your feet planted on the ground.
The word of God says pride goes before a fall.

Pride goeth before destruction, and an haughty spirit before a fall. – Proverbs 16:18

Success has levels. There are levels of success to climb while you walk and work
your way to becoming successful and great. Pride at one level of success can
halt or hinder you from climbing to the next higher level of success.

Your source remains God always. Men including you are but channels. Without
the source the channel can do nothing. When the channel gets cut off from
the source it dries up. Without God you can do nothing. Without Him I can
do nothing. Constant dependence on God is a must if you must have constant

success. Forgetting your source is a sure way to trip up and fall. Men have risen and fallen because they forgot where their strength comes from. Your strength comes from God. David recognized this and he never forgot this truth

My power and my strength come from the LORD and He has saved me- Psalm 118:14 CEV

Again in another place even though he was king- with much influence, riches, horses, servants and he himself was a warrior he had this to say

There is no king saved by the multitude of an host: a mighty man is not delivered by much strength. An horse is a vain thing for safety: neither shall he deliver any by his great strength. - Psalm 33:16-17

David never forgot what or who was the reason for his success. He acknowledged that it was God that gave him success when he had to fight the lions. His next victory was against the bear and again he gave God the glory for the victory. And now that he was confronted by Goliath he was confident that the God who made it possible for him to defeat the bear and the lion would also give him victory over Goliath.

David said moreover, The LORD that delivered me out of the paw of the lion, and out of the paw of the bear, he will deliver me out of the hand of this Philistine. And Saul said unto David, Go, and the LORD be with thee. – 1 Samuel 17:37

Without Him I can do nothing but with Him I can do all things through Christ that strengthens me.

I can do all things through Christ which strengtheneth me. – Philippians 4:13

Nothing is impossible for you when your strength comes from God. You are undefeatable if the strength of God is your strength. Before you succeed remember that God is the strength of your life. After you succeed still remember that He is the strength of your life. Without Him you are prey for the enemy. If God is not for you everything can and will be against you. Your success does not depend on anything you have or are rather it depends on God and His mighty power.

The horse is prepared for the day of battle but deliverance and victory are of the LORD- Proverbs 21:31 AMP.

The message translation of Proverbs 21:31 says it like this

Do your best, prepare for the worst- then trust God to bring victory- Proverbs 21:31 MSG

Your best minus God is not good enough to bring you victory, success and greatness. All your best efforts, your best strength, all your resources no matter how extensive they may be is not enough to make you successful and great. Add God to your best and you will continue to move from one level of success to another. Victory ALWAYS comes from God. Success ALWAYS comes from God. Greatness ALWAYS comes from God. He gives you power to be successful. So when you succeed at one level do not forget who made it possible for you to succeed. Remember your source and give Him the glory that He deserves. The song writer Fanny Crosby sang and said to God be the glory great things he has done.

Stay humble always. Pride pulls down fast. Pride happens when you refuse to acknowledge God as your source and are depending on men or yourself. That highly placed or influential uncle or aunt is not your source. He or she can be able to help you yet not be willing. It takes God who is the King of kings to make the king willing to help you for the king can be able yet not willing to help you.

In God is my salvation and my glory: the rock of my strength, and my refuge, is in God. Trust in him at all times; ye people, pour out your heart before him: God is a refuge for us. Surely men of low degree are vanity, and men of high degree are a lie: to be laid in the balance, they are altogether lighter than vanity. - Psalm 62:7-9

This is again King David in all his glory and might speaking. He acknowledges his constant dependence on God. Little wonder God describes David as a man after God's heart. This is a powerful king who never lost a war in his time. Yet he knows that even a king is powerless without the strength or power of God with him. Hear him- My soul, wait ONLY upon God.

My soul, wait thou only upon God; for my expectation is from him. He only is my rock and my salvation: he is my defence; I shall not be moved. Psalm 62:5-6

Pride acknowledges independence of God and acknowledges dependence on self. There was a man that was described as the rich fool in one parable. He had prospered and not once did he acknowledge God. He took the glory that belonged to God and it cost him dearly.

And he spake a parable unto them, saying, the ground of a certain rich man brought forth plentifully. And he thought within himself, saying, what shall I do, because I have no room where to bestow my fruits? And he said, this will I do: I will pull down my barns, and build greater; and there will I bestow all my fruits and my goods. And I will say to my soul, Soul, thou hast much goods laid up for many years; take thine ease, eat, drink, and be merry. But God said unto him, Thou fool, this night thy soul shall be required of thee: then whose shall those things be, which thou hast provided? – Luke 12:16-20

He mentioned the word "1" six times in four verses- verse 16-19. Not once did he mention God or acknowledge God. His ground brought forth plentifully but he failed to recognize the One who gave him the space in the earth to even plant seed that brought the harvest. We own nothing on this earth. Even the space to plant and reap a harvest is not yours. Everything belongs to God. Even the air you breathe belongs to God. The power to work comes from God alone. Six times in four verses he kept referring to himself and never mentioned God. He is a fool indeed. Who is a fool? The one who refuses to acknowledge God or that says that there is no God- *Psalm 53:1*. He was a proud person. In the fifth verse God answered and said to him- thou fool. A proud person is a fool and the end of fools is not good. May you not be called a fool by God. Amen!!

May your ground bring forth plentifully. May you succeed and become very successful but please for every level of success you reach don't forget who made it possible for you to succeed. Don't forget that it is God who made it possible for you to succeed. Climb up but keep your feet on the ground and stay humble. You will always need God so acknowledge your dependence on Him and stay dependent on Him always. Stay dependent on Him by staying humble even after you succeed. Lean on God totally.

It is much harder to stay humble and still dependent on God after you succeed than before you succeed. Almost anyone can be humble when they are down the ladder but when they have moved up the ladder it is hard though not impossible to stay humble. That is when you need to stay humble even more.

That is the time you need to remain even more dependent on God. The psalmist said- the LORD is my shepherd- *Psalm 23:1*. While passing through the valley the LORD remains his shepherd. When He has brought him through the valley of shadow of death He still remains his shepherd. No matter how big you get you can never be bigger than God. And you can never be too big not to need God.

Be careful when you reach the top. Recognize who is the source of your breakthroughs, success and greatness. To Him alone belongs the glory, worship and adoration. No man can make you because no man has ability to make another. He or she is mere flesh and blood just like you. He or she is just a channel or vessel. Don't give the praise that belongs to God to any man not even yourself. You set yourself up for failure when you give the glory that belongs to God to another.

Also after God has used you to be a channel of blessing don't take the glory that belongs to God. There are those that after you have been a blessing to them will want to carry the glory and give to you for what God had used you to do. They did so to Herod and it cost him his life. Don't allow anyone to kill you. King Herod allowed men to kill him when he took the glory that belonged to God.

And the assembled people shouted, it is the voice of a god, and not of a man! And at once an angel of the Lord smote him and cut him down, because he did not give God the glory (the preeminence and kingly majesty that belong to Him as the supreme Ruler); and he was eaten by worms and died. - Acts 12:22-23 AMP

The praise of men is a killer. It aborts destinies. It destroys men and keeps them from reaching where God planned for them to reach. You don't want to take the praise or glory that belongs to God. It belongs to God and to Him alone. He is a jealous God and His glory He will not share with another. Herod learned this the hard way.

Don't be like Herod who took the glory that belonged to God. His mistake and folly is our instruction and wisdom. We profit and learn wisdom from his folly. Nebuchadnezzar for a while lost his throne and his humanity because he did not give God the glory.

At the end of twelve months he walked in the palace of the kingdom of Babylon. The king spake, and said, is not this great Babylon, that I have built for the house of the kingdom by the might of my power, and for the honour of my majesty? – Daniel 4:29-30

Foolish king Nebuchadnezzar. He attempted to take the credit or the glory for what God had given him. Pride entered his head and God pulled him down fast:

While the word was in the king's mouth, there fell a voice from heaven, saying, O king Nebuchadnezzar, to thee it is spoken; The kingdom is departed from thee. And they shall drive thee from men, and thy dwelling shall be with the beasts of the field: they shall make thee to eat grass as oxen, and seven times shall pass over thee, until thou know that the most High ruleth in the kingdom of men, and giveth it to whomsoever he will. – Daniel 4:31-32

However his case was better than that of Herod in Acts 12. He learned a valuable lesson from this experience for in the end this is what Nebuchadnezzar said:

And at the end of the days I Nebuchadnezzar lifted up mine eyes unto heaven, and mine understanding returned unto me, and I blessed the most High, and I praised and honored him that liveth forever, whose dominion is an everlasting dominion, and his kingdom is from generation to generation.- Daniel 4:34

The honor and glory he refused to give God in the first place he had learned to give and promptly too. He goes on to give good advice. His experience teaches him that God is able to abase the proud person whether you are king or peasant. Don't forget the source of all your breakthrough, achievement and success.

Now I Nebuchadnezzar praise and extol and honour the King of heaven, all whose works are truth, and his ways judgment: and those that walk in pride he is able to abase. – Daniel 4:37

The word of God says we should not forget that He (God) gives us power to become anything that is useful or significant- *Deuteronomy 8:18.*

But thou shalt remember the LORD thy God: for it is he that giveth thee power to get wealth that he may establish his covenant which he sware unto thy fathers, as it is this day.

Victory, success and greatness is yours but the glory for the victory, success and greatness is not yours. Take the victory but let God take the glory. Don't let the praise of men get to your head. It can pull you down. Beware of the praise of men. After you succeed give the glory to God. When you have become great give the glory to God. When (not if) you have achieved success give Him all the glory. Don't even attempt to share his glory. Without him you can do nothing. It's not your skill. It is not your qualification. Better believe it there are several out there that are more qualified than you who did not succeed. It is the grace of God. Don't take the glory for the miracles He does through you. You are only a vessel. The power and the authority is from God.

We have this treasure from God, but we are like clay jars that hold the treasure. This shows that the great power is from God, not from us. - 2 Corinthians 4:7 NCV

Men praised Herod. He accepted the praise of men. He soaked it (the praises) in. He lost his throne and his life. They said he was God. He got filled with pride. And his fall started. Don't allow men to turn you to God. There is nothing you accomplish that will not be by the grace of God. There is nothing you can do if God did not give you the life and the ability to do it. Accept thank you from men but give God the glory always.

And lead us not into temptation, but deliver us from evil: For thine is the kingdom, and the power, and the glory, forever. Amen. – Matthew 6:13

Don't allow anybody to kill you. All glory belongs to God. Thine (God) is the glory. The glory always belongs to God and never to us. When you have done well for people accept their thanks but don't take the glory or the praise for what God did through you. You are just a vessel. The power comes from God. Know what belongs to you and what belongs to God. Accept appreciation from men but don't take the praise and the glory that belongs to God. It can hurt you. Beware of the praise of men. It can destroy. It can terminate your destiny and even your life. So always remember that to Him alone belongs the glory. Before you succeed and become great remember that the glory belongs to Him. While you are succeeding and on your way up remember that the glory belongs to Him. And when you get to the top remember that always the glory belongs to Him.

When you succeed and you will succeed let your testimony or confession be like that of the apostle Paul who said:

And they glorified God [as the Author and Source of what had taken place] in me. - Galatians 1:24 AMP

No man takes the glory for the great and wonderful things God has done and will do in your life. When you forget to give the glory to God you forfeit the blessing. All not some of the glory belongs to God. You are nothing without Him or without His grace. Paul said yes I worked more than most yet it is His grace more than anything that has made me who I am. It is His grace that has brought me this far. His grace empowered me to do all that I have done.

But by the grace of God I am what I am: and his grace which was bestowed upon me was not in vain; but I labored more abundantly than they all: yet not I, but the grace of God which was with me. – 1 Corinthians 15:10

The apostle Paul said they glorified God as the author and source of all that had taken place in him. Men glorified God for what they had seen happen through the hands of Paul. We are instruments for God. The instrument wields no power without the person who holds it. The axe cannot swing itself. We are but battle axes in the hands of Almighty God. We should never forget that if we want to continue to succeed in life. No matter how sharp the axe is it cannot swing itself. The power to swing and cut comes from the one who holds it and swings it (the axe).

Don't take the glory and don't allow anybody to give you the glory for what God has done through you. You are just a vessel. Beware of the praise of men. It has destroyed the work of the hands of many. It has even consumed the lives of some for God is a jealous God and His glory He will not give to another. He will not even share it with you.

God deserves the glory and should get the glory. Paul declared that he is what he is by the grace of God. Yes he put in some energy, experience, time, perhaps money and ability. Still the glory belongs to him alone. In all your achievement whether small or big only God deserves the glory. If His power must be made available for your next level then you must give Him the glory for your present level. Thanksgiving and giving Him all the glory in your present level will set you up for your next level.

In God and by God you will succeed and you will become great but you must never forget to return glory to the One who demands and deserves the glory- Jehovah God is His name. Be like Paul and say

But by the grace of God I am what I am: and his grace which was bestowed upon me was not in vain; but I laboured more abundantly than they all: yet not I, but the grace of God which was with me. – 1 Corinthians 15:10

10

THE CONCLUSION OF THE MATTER

Build your life on your dreams; because dreams
never have bad endings- M.F. Moonzajer

Let us hear the conclusion of the whole matter: Fear God, and keep his
commandments: for this is the whole duty of man. - Ecclesiastes 12:13

King Solomon who is the wisest man the earth had ever known before Christ
walked the earth said let us hear the conclusion of the matter. What is the
conclusion of this matter? Fear (honor, reverence, respect) God, obey Him,
delight in Him, love Him and serve Him. He has a plan for your life. He has
a plan for your success and greatness. He wants you to succeed and be great.
There is the **world** way to succeed and there is the **WORD** way to succeed and
become great. True or godly success and greatness without God is impossible.
Following God and the way of God will bring you into success and greatness.

The conclusion of the matter is that success and greatness is not reserved for a
few. God did not plan that some would be successful and many will be failures.
You too can succeed in every area of life that God has called you into. Greatness
is possible. You can become successful and great because God has planted the
seeds for success and greatness inside you. There is a winner in you. When
you identify the winner in you God will help you to unleash the winner in
you. The conclusion of the matter is that no excuse is excusable for you not to
succeed and become great. If you will pay the price you will possess the prize
of success and greatness.

Your present level is not good enough and so God is empowering you to
move beyond your present level to your next level. Your progress will not stop

until you reach the topmost top. Gideon will no longer thresh wheat rather he will thrash Midianites of opposition, poverty, sickness and disease. Sons and daughters of God will no longer be pursued. The pursued are turning to pursuers. The hunted are turning to the hunter.

These are the last days. The days for unleashing the sons and daughters of God. Days in which God is raining down His spirit upon all His children. We are living in the days that the sons and daughters of God will tear every leash that has kept them bound and limited so that they can reach out for success and greatness. We will no longer be held down rather we will spread our wings and fly. God gave us wings to fly and we will fly high to the glory of God. We will march on and conquer territories for God. By faith we will march ahead to shine our light and destroy the works of darkness. We are the ones the word of God calls saviors.

Then saviors shall come to Mount Zion to judge the mountains of Esau, and the kingdom shall be the LORD's. - Obadiah 1:21

Saviors or deliverers that will be battle axes in the hands of God to deliver the world from the bondage of sin and the curse of sin. They will judge sickness, failure, depression and all works of the enemy that Christ the Savior has already saved mankind from. However as we enlist in this end time push for God we must vow to give God the glory always.

Congratulations beloved of God. This is your season to manifest success and greatness. It's you season to succeed, succeed, succeed and to move towards greatness. It's your turn to be blessed indeed. And you will be blessed. You will manifest great success and uncommon greatness. Yes by the power of the most High God that dwells in you it is so. You will unleash your full potential in God. It was settled at Calvary. You will unleash greatness from inside you.

Remember that all you have done is not all you can do! Unleash all of your potential in God. Unleash the greatness in you. Loose the winner in you.

Start to succeed. Continue to succeed until you become very successful and great. God created you for success and greatness. So dare to move towards success and greatness. You have already been wired for success and greatness by God. God has planted inside you seeds of success and greatness. Inside you lies the ingredients for success and greatness. It's time to unleash the success and greatness that lies hidden inside you. There is a giant inside you. Unleash the giant inside you. There is a warrior inside you. Unleash the warrior inside you. There is a winner in you. Unleash the winner in you. The principles outlined in this book and founded on the word of God will help you unleash the winner in you. Your success is important to God and that is why He planted the potential for success and greatness inside you. It is time to unleash all of that potential inside you. And you will because that is the will of God for you.

God helped Gideon unleash the warrior inside him. If you are a saint of God then you have the same God that Gideon had. What God did for Gideon He will do for you if you will trust Him and walk with Him. God took 12 lowly and unknown fishermen and turned them to famous world beaters.

And when they found them not, they drew Jason and certain brethren unto the rulers of the city, crying, these that have turned the world upside down are come hither also- Acts 17:6 KJV

You have been beaten by the world too long. You have been beaten by Midianites of sickness, scarcity, drugs, immorality, failure, debt and everything that the cross of Christ paid to set you free from. Turnaround time is come. It is time for the pursued to turn pursuer. The prey is turning to the predator. We are taking territories for God. It is time for God to turn you to a world beater and this He will do because He that called you is faithful. God is unleashing His kingdom on the kingdom of darkness. These are the days wherein God is unleashing the sons of God on their world. Sons are rising up to take their proper place. You are one of such sons and daughters of the kingdom that will be battle axes or instruments in the hands of God to set the captives free. There is a warrior inside you. There is a winner inside you. Success and greatness lies inside you. **Unleash the winner in you**. The One who called you is faithful and He will do it.

Faithful is he that calleth you, who also will do it. - 1 Thessalonians 5:24

TO GOD BE THE GLORY ALWAYS

Printed in the United States
By Bookmasters